M000285663

CLIMBING
your way to
WEALTH

CLIMBING
your way to
WEALTH

HOW TO NAVIGATE YOUR RETIREMENT

RICH LIBERANTE

CFP®, CPA, Masters in Tax

Advantage®

Published by Advantage, Charleston, South Carolina.
Member of Advantage Media Group.

ADVANTAGE is a registered trademark, and the Advantage colophon is a trademark of Advantage Media Group, Inc.

Printed in the United States of America.

10 9 8 7 6 5 4 3 2 1

ISBN: 978-1-64225-228-6
LCCN: 2020913379

Cover design by Carly Blake.
Layout design by Wesley Strickland.

This publication is designed to provide accurate and authoritative information in regard to the subject matter covered. It is sold with the understanding that the publisher is not engaged in rendering legal, accounting, or other professional services. If legal advice or other expert assistance is required, the services of a competent professional person should be sought.

 Advantage Media Group is proud to be a part of the Tree Neutral® program. Tree Neutral offsets the number of trees consumed in the production and printing of this book by taking proactive steps such as planting trees in direct proportion to the number of trees used to print books. To learn more about Tree Neutral, please visit **www.treeneutral.com**.

Advantage Media Group is a publisher of business, self-improvement, and professional development books and online learning. We help entrepreneurs, business leaders, and professionals share their Stories, Passion, and Knowledge to help others Learn & Grow. Do you have a manuscript or book idea that you would like us to consider for publishing? Please visit **advantagefamily.com** or call **1.866.775.1696**.

CONTENTS

THE LAY OF THE LAND

I don't know where you are right now. Maybe you're sitting in a library or a bookstore, having just purchased this book. Perhaps you're at home, comfy on the sofa, or squeezed onto the train during a long commute. Wherever you are, I want you to pause for a moment, close your eyes, and imagine you're somewhere else.

The first thing you notice about this new place is the bitter cold. It's more extreme than any bad winter weather you've ever experienced, and it cuts through you with each persistent gust of wind.

That's the second thing: the wind, which constantly threatens to blow you over. The noise of it is so loud that you can barely hear yourself think. Particles of what you assume to be snow fleck your face, but you have never known snow to sting so sharply. It feels like handfuls of sand are being fired at you from a jet engine. The wind and the blinding, jagged snow make it nearly impossible to see what's around you—the whole world appears to be a featureless void of white.

Any ideas yet?

The unrelenting weather forces you to duck into a tent to protect yourself. It's so small that you can't stand up, but the deeply driven stakes keep it from flying away with you inside, like a frosty Dorothy in *The Wizard of Oz*. It's much warmer in the tent, thanks to a tiny portable stove providing heat. And when you slip into your sleeping bag, rated to below -20°, it will become even cozier.

You share this tent with a number of other shivering bodies. These are your teammates, your coworkers, your fellow travelers. You know little about them, beyond basic biographical details, but you have already put your life in their hands.

Have you figured it out yet? How about a few more clues:

When the snow clears and the sun starts to rise, you will get up and load your gear as quickly as possible. Every second counts in this place, and a few extra minutes wasted fussing with outerwear or a pack could mean the difference between success or ultimate failure. You researched and strategized and prognosticated for months—maybe years—to select the right moment to make your move, and your window of opportunity will be pitilessly small. Despite this, you will force yourself to move slowly and patiently because the only thing more dangerous here than losing time is making mistakes.

Know where you are? You are in one of the most infamous places on earth that most humans will never actually see: Base Camp of Mount Everest. You may be justified wondering what Mount Everest could possibly have to do with managing your retirement. After all, it's hard to think of two more divergent worlds than high-stakes adventure mountaineering and the vital, but often quite dry, realm of financial planning. I've been working as a financial planner for twenty-four years, however, and in that time, I've realized that Everest provides an uncannily accurate metaphor for our financial lives.

Climbing Mount Everest is an epic undertaking and, for many people who make the attempt, it is a once-in-a-lifetime experience. It is also extremely risky, and survival—let alone success—is by no means assured.

Everest is also an apt metaphor because all too often, people put all their focus on the wrong elements of the endeavor. Ask any experienced mountaineer, and they will tell you that the most challenging and critically important part of the whole effort is getting *down* from the peak. Yet how do we talk about Everest? It's always "climbing," "scaling," and "reaching the top," as though the effort ends when we plant our flag at twenty-nine thousand feet. People make the same mistake when thinking about their financial health: they spend most of their time thinking about what the financial industry calls "the accumulation phase" and very little time strategizing about everything that comes after.

Think of the accumulation phase as the trip up the mountain. This is the time in your life when you are working and creating wealth, getting closer and closer to retirement—the "peak" of the financial mountain. A lot of advice and common wisdom about money management focuses on this part of the process as well. We are bombarded with messages about earning and investing and returns, and generally *getting to* retirement, but there's very little information widely available about how to actually retire in a safe and comfortable way. This leaves way too many people arriving at the pinnacle of their journey—retirement—and breathing a sigh of relief, only to realize that they have no clear plan for funding or even filling the next twenty or thirty years of their lives.

But that's the thing about mountains and about our lives—both are subject to that unbreakable law of physics: what goes up must come down. And it is in that journey down that even experienced and prepared mountaineers can run into trouble. When you are coming down the mountain, there's a lot working against you. You have spent a lot of energy getting up the mountain and experienced the ongoing strain of laboring at high altitudes. *Every* kind of resource is more limited on the descent, including the most precious resource of all:

> *Every* kind of resource is more limited on the descent, including the most precious resource of all: time.

time. You only have so many hours of good visibility in which to make it back to the safety of base camp, and staying put is not an option.

When it comes to our financial lives, the dangers of the descent are more abstract and less physical, but many of the same principles hold true. Retirement represents a sudden limiting of our resources and puts us on a restrictive timeline. When we stop working, we enter the "disbursement phase," where we draw upon our store of wealth without replacing or building it. With no new income, we have only whatever we have managed to accumulate on the "climb" to get us safely and comfortably to the end of our journey. Like climbers who are wearied after the rigors of the ascent, by the time we retire, we are also usually ready for a rest, and we are less willing or able to generate more income if necessary.

But even though our resources are stretched more thinly, we still have to get down the same amount of mountain that we just climbed. When we retire, our lives don't immediately shift into low-income mode; we still have bills and obligations and wants and needs. The only difference is that now we have a clearly finite amount of wealth available to meet not only our needs for today and tomorrow but possibly for the next two or three decades. Everything must be carefully planned and assets repositioned for a challenging journey. This kind of specific planning is a skill, and it's one that most people haven't cultivated because, up until this point, they haven't really needed it. Instead, they've been focusing on getting better and better at climbing up a mountain. Now, for the first time, they have to figure out how to climb down, and they have to do it on the fly. Most importantly, they have to do it right the first time because there will only be one chance to make their descent.

The journey back down isn't just more difficult, however; it's also more dangerous. For the most part, if you make a mistake going up a mountain, you can compensate and keep moving. A delay or an equipment malfunction may rob you of some precious time and energy, but usually, you can improvise a solution and keep going. On the descent, however, there is no slack and no flexibility. If you lose time, you run into the immovable and deadly nightfall. If you fall or damage your equipment, you may not have the physical energy required to recover or any replacement materials left. The margin of error is razor thin, and the consequences for failure are dire.

Again, we see this dynamic reflected in our financial lives as well. When we are young and able-bodied with current skills and lots of time, the occasional bad investment or unexpected expense might slow us down or cramp our lifestyle for a few years, but recovery is possible. We can make more money, our investments can garner further returns, we can adjust our portfolios and meet our financial obligations because we have that cushion of time and resources. When we reach retirement age, every setback and mistake becomes less manageable. Losing 30 percent on a bad investment when you're thirty means a bad few years; losing that same 30 percent at age sixty could seriously impact the rest of your life.

One of the biggest dangers of the descent both in climbing and in savings is the psychological impact of all these other risk factors.

When you are standing on the precipice and it occurs to you that you need to get all the way back down, you suddenly become acutely aware of all the other problems we've just discussed. You can feel the cold in your bones and the fog in your head. You think ruefully of the meager remaining oxygen tanks you have and of the extra rope you used up on a difficult clamber earlier. You look at the angle of the sun and realize your visibility will soon be reduced. Similarly, so many people reach or approach retirement only to realize that their accumulated assets won't cover their current lifestyle for as long as they'd assumed. Or maybe that the 401(k) they cashed out a few years ago did more damage than they'd realized, or any of the other numerous uncomfortable surprises that can crop up when you switch from looking at your wealth with an accumulation mindset to seeing it with an eye toward distribution. And suddenly, people see long years and a lot of uncertainty stretching out before them, and they feel fear—maybe not for their physical safety, but real fear nonetheless.

Psychologically, this fear can be another major danger for people approaching retirement. Though the accumulation phase, much like the ascent up a mountain, can have its challenges and perils, there's a sense of excitement and achievement that pushes us onward. Being able to recover from those roadblocks bolsters our self-esteem and only strengthens our resolve to make it to the top. Heading downward, however, that powerful incentive is gone. We no longer feel like we are working toward an achievement but that we're just trying to survive a journey. This deflating feeling can lead to one of the worst things you can do, either as a mountaineer or a retiree: panic.

Panic is what causes otherwise staid professionals to move too fast and to take risks they never would have taken when "climbing." Panic clouds our judgment and can lead to a cascade of bad choices that sends us tumbling off into oblivion. Like the climber who tries to beat the clock by moving dangerously fast, a retiree who decides to suddenly pour his assets into a volatile get-rich-quick scheme may find that their reaction to the perceived risk was actually more dangerous—and more destructive—than the original bad situation. There is an undeniable urgency that comes with the "descent," and it's natural to feel a strong urge to move quickly and seize what can appear to be the only remaining opportunities, especially if you don't feel you've fully prepared for this moment in your life. Unfortunately, the things we want to do least—strategize carefully and move with deliberation—are the most important.

This panic effect is amplified for people approaching retirement because while no one is ever going to just wake up and find themselves on top of a mountain, the peaks of our financial lives have a way of sneaking up on us. Many, many clients come to me not even having realized they've passed the summit and are heading down the other side. Often, this means that for months or years, they have been making errors, both small and large, without ever realizing what was going on. Can you imagine how bad you would be at getting *down* a mountain if you believed you were still climbing it? Realizing that your financial situation is fundamentally different than you'd assumed is a huge source of anxiety for people and often leads them to scramble for solutions when what they really need to do is take a breath and make a plan.

It's easy to say that, of course, when it's not your butt hanging off the side of a mountain—or your money being gobbled up by retirement expenses. This brings me to possibly the most important way in which the experience of climbing Mount Everest is like our financial lives: *it always goes better if you have an experienced guide.*

The history of the Sherpa people of northern Tibet is so closely intertwined with that of Everest—or Chomolungma, as they have called it for hundreds of years—that their proximity to the mountain has altered their very DNA. Sherpa people often have unique physiological features, including greater lung capacity, more rapid and deeper breathing, and enhanced blood circulation, among other characteristics. These are markers, geneticists believe, of the people's physical adaptations to the high-altitude environment in which they've made their homes for generations. This means that in addition to strong cultural and religious traditions that involve understanding the mountain and the area in general, many Sherpas are also more physically capable of surviving the conditions on Everest.

Sherpa men and women also hold a number of world records related to the mountain, including the youngest people to summit, the youngest women (both aged sixteen), the only person to summit twice in a single climbing session, and numerous other achievements. Yet mountaineering is hardly intrinsic to Sherpa culture. Without the economic incentives—and pressure—of Western mountaineers, the Sherpa likely would have had little interest in climbing the peak they refer to as "the mother of the world."

Sherpa people became involved in the business of Everest largely because of proximity. Foreign climbers, most notably Sir Edmund Hillary, hired local Sherpa farmers to help carry supplies on their exploratory trips up the mountain. It was through this association that individual Sherpas began to demonstrate a unique mountaineering skill—an aptitude for altitude, if you will.

This relationship has been a double-edged sword for the Sherpa community in the shadow of Everest, especially as the mountain becomes more and more commercialized and more popular. Sherpas pick up the slack on an expedition and bear a heavy burden—often quite literally. They have to do what would be, for many, the athletic feat of a lifetime (climbing Mount Everest) while also transporting many of the necessary supplies and guiding a group of people with variable levels of experience and skill. In fact, they often do even more climbing than just a single trip to the top, moving forward to set lines and prepare the way for customers before descending to lead the group upward again.

In addition to carrying more of the literal weight of these expeditions, Sherpas also absorb a lot of the danger of the expedition. Almost half of all deaths on Everest in the modern era have been Sherpas. Their names are rarely, if ever, mentioned, and their roles often elided, but make no mistake: almost no one sees the top of Mount Everest without the assistance of a Sherpa. Whether it's help with carrying supplies or preparing climbing materials or, as in some notable cases, literally being "towed" up part of the mountain, summiting Mount Everest is a team effort, and a Sherpa's expertise is a critical part of the process.

I am not a Sherpa. My relationship with my clients doesn't put me at nearly the same risks, and I have the enormous luxury of not having to go through my clients' experiences along with them. I do, however, think of myself as uniquely adapted for the unusual atmosphere of retirement and well prepared to guide others through the process. I may not be saving you from a long fall off a mountain, but I can make sure you have the most comfortable and freeing retirement possible.

There are a lot of financial advisors in the world, many of them quite good, but the vast majority of them do not specialize in managing retirement. Most financial advisors—just like most forms of financial advice—focus on the accumulation phase. It makes sense. Everyone wants to grow their wealth; it's an exciting topic that is easy to sell. In comparison, the slower and more complicated process of projecting and structuring that wealth for your retirement and beyond can seem distant, less urgent, and a lot less fun. It's also a lot easier as a young person just starting in their career to pitch themselves as someone who can help clients save or earn more, rather than simply asking people to put their entire nest egg in the hands of a twenty-five-year-old.

What this means practically is that many people, even people who have seen a financial advisor in the past, have almost never actually worked with a retirement expert. Many people even assume that retirement experts don't really exist or are superfluous and that if someone can handle the accumulation phase, they're probably equipped to do everything else. To return to our mountain metaphor, this would be like presuming that because the nice salesman at REI can give you good advice on which hiking boots to buy, he could probably help you reach the summit of Everest too.

At my company, Watermark Wealth Strategies, our goal is to provide comprehensive planning services. We offer everything you need to get from base camp to back home safely, all in one company. To do this, we have developed a diversity of skills, both in terms of the experts we employ and the actual breadth of experience and knowledge that each team member possesses. The team that gets someone to the top of Mount Everest isn't just the Sherpa and the climber; there are also the professional consultants who help plan and execute each trip, the logistical experts who get you to and from the mountain, and the support staff at base camp who troubleshoot during the trip. All these people and more work together to accomplish one of the most notable feats of human adventure.

I say "adventure" because this is the place where the Everest analogy really departs from our financial life: climbing Mount Everest is a choice. For some people, it may certainly feel like a compulsion. Like Sir Edmund Hillary, certain people do feel a need to climb mountains simply "because they are there," but for most of us, we could happily live our entire lives never going above sea level. Retiring, on the other hand, is not optional. Even if you wanted to stay in the accumulation phase forever, most of us are forced to quit working eventually, either by logistical or physiological factors. In that way, it is a little bit like waking up on the tip-top of a mountain—maybe we didn't want to be there, and maybe we don't want to go down; maybe we're even afraid and don't feel all that confident in our mountaineering skills, but we don't have the luxury of staying still.

One way or another, we all have to get down the mountain. My goal, both with this book and in my work at Watermark Wealth Strategies, is to help people have the safest, most positive descent possible, and that's going to look a bit different for every person. Everyone brings something a little different to the mountain—some people have the finest equipment money can buy, while other people have to make do with blue-light specials. Some climbers are more skilled than others or benefit from more experience. Some are lucky enough to get clear weather for their descent, and others have to face the storm. A good guide can weigh all of these factors and develop a route down that capitalizes on each individual climber's strengths and mitigates their weaknesses.

It's easy to feel isolated on the top of a mountain. The howling of the wind makes communication difficult, and reduced visibility can narrow your world to a pinpoint. It's tempting to believe, in that situation, that the only thing you can rely on is yourself and that you should just forge ahead in whatever direction seems clearest. In reality, that's a pretty good way to fall off a mountain. Even at the top of the world—even at the most critical transition points of our lives—we are not alone. There are experts, there are guides, there are answers, and, perhaps even more importantly, there are people who know the right questions to ask.

Mountaineering, like many other hobbies, has its own specialized lingo used to describe concepts specific to the sport. In that parlance, "beta" means information about a climb, sought or given before the climber actually attempts it. "Running beta" is the act of getting that information while actively climbing—it is learning and doing, all rolled into one. Think of this book as a form of financial "running beta." We are all in the midst of our personal fiscal journey, and some are closer to the tipping point than others, but it's never too late to gather more information about the terrain beneath our feet.

CHAPTER ONE:

LIFE IS TOUGHER ON THIS SIDE OF THE MOUNTAIN

Most people don't realize it, but wealth has a life cycle just like any other living thing. It's not stagnant; it's certainly not constant, but it is somewhat predictable. The cycle of wealth in most people's lives begins with something we've discussed in the first chapter: accumulation. We could think of this as "climbing the mountain," but it's really more like *building* a mountain.

The accumulation phase starts when we first begin accruing assets for use in retirement. For most of us, this means our first job, where we begin earning wealth, paying a portion of our income toward Social Security, and, if possible, buying and funding investment products like 401(k)s or IRAs. A lucky few might start sooner with ancestral wealth or savings products started in childhood by parents, but most of us have just those same four or five decades to earn and save everything we can.

Time is our greatest asset during the accumulation phase (second only to, well, great assets). Generally, the longer money sits in an investment product, the more value it will accrue, and extra time also gives investors more flexibility when it comes to allocating their portfolios. People with another thirty years of incoming money can afford to be more aggressive or experimental with their money than people with only five or ten more working years.

The accumulation stage is important, and it is big—it will occupy roughly half of your life—but, in many ways, it's the "easiest" part of the financial life cycle. Not that earning money is necessarily "easy," as any working person can attest, but it is straightforward, almost automatic in many aspects. Your contributions to Social Security, for example, happen without any effort on your part, and many jobs include easy opt-in 401(k)s or IRAs that automatically debit from your paychecks. You could be quite passive during the accumulation phase and still establish a solid nest egg for yourself just with these types of saving vehicles.

In fact, most people don't do much portfolio management during this time—according to a recent survey, more than 42 percent of investors don't actually know how their money is allocated.[1] And having *any* money invested at all puts these people significantly ahead of the average in America, where nearly half of all working families have no retirement savings at all.[2] For many people, the "accumulation phase" is more like the "keeping your head above water phase," and it tends to last well through any nominal retirement. If you have

---

1   "2018 Retirement Preparedness Survey: A Generational Challenge," Prudential, 2019, https://www.prudential.com/wps/wcm/connect/cc6944cd-777c-4dcd-b7f2-0858e2514b39/Retirement-Dream-is-Becoming-More-Elusive.pdf?MOD=AJPERES&CVID=mC.uNZ9.

2   Monique Morrissey, "The State of American Retirement: How 401(k)s Have Failed Most American Workers," Economic Policy Institute, March 3, 2016, https://www.epi.org/publication/retirement-in-america/#charts.

savings and are reading this book because you want to know how best to use them in retirement, that alone puts you significantly ahead of the curve.

The primary overriding principle of the accumulation phase is, as you might expect, to accumulate. If you are spending less money than you are making, you are doing it "right." I usually recommend my clients aim to save or invest no less than 10 percent of their gross income, though 30 percent is really the sweet spot in terms of building a lot of wealth. If you do that, you pay yourself first and do what you want with the remainder, and you'll still be in a good position when you get ready to retire.

Of course, if I were advising a client on the ideal way to structure their extra income, there are numerous other things I could recommend over lots of luxury timepieces or expensive cars, but at its core, this is all the accumulation phase really demands. Most people can handle that pretty intuitively—in fact, for a large swath of the population, that's all "managing your money" really means. Accumulation also relies most heavily upon earning income—the bulk of our wealth is made that way, rather than through pure asset allocation. This means that people can be successful during the accumulation phase simply by focusing on their job, the thing they are most fully trained and educated to do. When it comes to the distribution phase, however, specialized knowledge isn't just helpful—it's necessary.

The distribution phase typically begins with retirement, but more broadly, it starts whenever we start consistently drawing upon our pool of resources more than we replenish it. The distribution phase ends when we do, and the last phase—the legacy phase—deals with any assets that might remain after our passing. The distribution phase was once relatively brief, compared to the ones that precede and follow it, but as the average human life span has expanded, so has the time we spend not working but still living our lives. Now, we might need income in retirement for twenty-five, or thirty, or even thirty-five years—nearly as long as we spent working—and the longer this phase goes on, the more difficult it is to manage comfortably. For example, my father is now going into his thirty-second year of retirement!

The accumulation phase is all about forward momentum—all you need to do is focus on growth. Distribution is about balance. You need to manage your daily expenses, understand how people spend in retirement, and maintain a large enough pool of assets for a projected future, which puts you in a fulcrum position, with today and tomorrow on either end of the see-saw.

The difference between the phases is probably best exemplified by the role that returns play in each. In the accumulation phase, all you really care about is your average rate of return. If you can look at your statements every year and see that your investments are growing at a respectable rate of, say, 7.6 or 8.2 percent, you can feel confident that things are going well. If you were to check in on your investments every month rather than every year, you would see that your steady 7.6 percent growth is actually a hodgepodge of fluctuations that might be anywhere from -18 percent to +22 percent. Time flattens out these peaks and gullies and gives you that long-term average return rate. When you retire and start pulling money from those investments, however, you are going to have to pick a specific month and year to start doing that, and you will only have limited control over when that happens.

This is particularly important because our investments don't just have short-term fluctuations; they are distinct periods of low or high rates of return that often last years or even decades. You might be able to delay your disbursement phase a bit to avoid starting in a low month, but if you happen to retire in a bad year (or years), you don't have many options. Even in recent decades, we've seen several periods in the market when unlucky retirees lost a lot of their wealth simply because of when they entered their disbursement stage.

One of the best examples of this problem in action is a concept called dollar cost averaging—this is a specific type of strategy where you buy or fund an investment at the same rate over time. For example, you might own a mutual fund, and you decide you are going to put $200 into it every two weeks. With market fluctuations, however, $200 doesn't always buy you the same number of shares. If the market is doing poorly, your contribution will buy more shares than in a more robust period. Investing a fixed amount on a regular basis allows you to capitalize on the lulls and "buy low" while avoiding the risks inherent in trying to time the market, and the longer you do this, the closer you get to a comfortable average growth.

If you reverse this process—as you will when you start taking income from your investments—the benefits of dollar cost averaging become challenges to overcome. If you start withdrawing $200 a month from that same mutual fund, you will quickly find that some withdrawals require more shares to be sold than others. If you are relying exclusively on that mutual fund to provide your monthly income, you may find yourself being forced to sell or liquidate assets at a lower rate than you'd like. If the market is doing poorly, this could take a bigger chunk out of your nest egg very early into retirement.

The worst part of all of this is that money lost in early retirement typically isn't recoverable. When someone coined the phrase "You never get a second chance at a first impression," they probably weren't thinking about retirement financing, but it is apt nonetheless. If you retire into a time of negative returns, you could later have ten years of solid 8 percent returns, and your asset growth still wouldn't catch up to someone who started their retirement in a booming—or even just a positive—market.

This is a scary thought for most of us because you could theoretically do everything else right and still get hammered simply by bad timing. The good news is that this problem is well understood by financial advisors who specialize in retirement like myself, and there are ways to manage or reduce this risk. Unlike the average person who only has this experience once in their life, we have guided countless clients through the process of retirement in all types of market conditions.

> A lot of people are inching toward this major life change without realizing it is happening or that they actually do need an expert to navigate it safely.

The average person does not have the benefit of that experience, and most people outside the financial industry simply don't know about a lot of the best strategies to keep their assets safe during the disbursement phase. This is totally normal—after all, this is my job; I am paid to know these things, just like you might be paid to know all about leading a corporation or designing architecture or performing neurosurgery. The problem is that a lot of people are inching toward this major life change without realizing it is happening or that they actually do need an expert to navigate it safely.

People who have done particularly well in terms of amassing wealth can struggle with this quite a bit. Because they have seen great success as a result of their financial choices, they've come to think of themselves as "good with money," and maybe they are—they are certainly good at making it. But disbursement often requires people to go against the instincts that made them wealthy in the first place, and it demands a level of foreknowledge that even the savviest layperson just doesn't have. It reminds me a bit of the type of kid we all knew (or maybe even were) in high school who always sailed easily to the top of the class without putting forth much effort. That kid often had a long struggle ahead of them when they got to college and discovered that the standards and demands were much different and more rigorous.

I share this information with you not to disparage people who take a DIY approach to retirement—it's certainly not some moral wrong, and many of our clients grew up in a generation or economic class where it was commonly expected that people would handle their money by themselves. Instead, I want to explain to you how much better retirement *could* be. One of the biggest problems with going it alone through the disbursement phase is that even if you make it through more or less unscathed, you will never know how much more you could have gotten out of your accumulated wealth.

To give you an example: I see many clients who come to me a couple of years before they plan to retire with a large chunk of savings in traditional IRAs. Often, they were eligible to convert those funds into a Roth IRA at a very lost cost years before but hadn't taken that opportunity for whatever reason. This is critical, because the money in a traditional IRA is taxed when you take it *out*, while the money in a Roth is taxed when you make your initial contribution or conversion. For people approaching retirement, this difference is especially important because many people shift tax brackets as they age and get closer to the disbursement phase. Most people wind up in a higher tax bracket at some point of their life due to the death of one spouse, and they thus would pay more in taxes upon withdrawing the money than they would have spending it earlier in their lives. My clients who missed their window to convert their traditional IRAs could end up paying more in taxes for no real reason other than a lack of knowledge about their options.

The problem is this: you don't know what you don't know. You might be surprised, even shocked, to learn that there is a part of the climb high up on Everest that routinely hits 100° during the day. It is called the Western Cwm (pronounced "coom"). Because of its unique valley structure, there is little wind, and the intense sunlight bouncing off the ice routinely heats the air to over 100°F. I can imagine that if you were not forewarned about this, it would never, ever cross your mind as even a possibility on the frozen mountain.

> **The problem is this: you don't know what you don't know.**

Our financial health is a lot like our physical health: at different ages, we are exposed to different risks, and we don't always get an obvious warning when our needs and capabilities are changing. Someone could be a passionate runner, logging marathons and training constantly for years, and they might assume that they were in perfect health. But behavior that was great for them at twenty maybe isn't the ideal option at forty-five—maybe running puts too much stress on joints or discs as their body ages, and a less aggressive form of exercise would actually be better for their overall health.

Similarly, our health goals and financial goals both have a way of slowly shifting without us necessarily realizing it. I have sat down with so many clients who were nearing retirement but had the kind of aggressive, risky portfolio I would only recommend for a high earner in their early career. People spend so long in "accumulation mode," thinking almost exclusively about how to bring in more money, that they don't notice when the risks of their strategies start to outweigh the benefits. Like the runner who keeps pushing for a shorter mile or longer marathons while inching closer and closer to a slipped disc, investors can get so focused on growth that they don't see how close to the precipice they really are. Like a climber with Everest fever, they see dangers mounting but press on toward the summit when all signs around them are pointing to turn back.

When I see a client in that situation, I usually ask them to do a little thought experiment. I ask them to imagine they have a really good year based on their current investments—maybe they make an extra $50,000 or even $100,000—and I ask them how that would materially change their life in retirement. Most people reply with some variation of "not much." People who have been very successful in accumulation have often already reached a level at which they have the things they need and want, and additional wealth has only a negligible impact on their daily life. Then, I ask them how their lives would change if they lost an equivalent amount of wealth at the beginning of their retirement. That idea almost always makes people pause to consider how much a big loss like that would curtail their plans and make their future insecure. Put in those terms, clients usually realize that their circumstances have changed, and their thinking and strategizing has to change as well.

There's no shame in not having this knowledge. Every running enthusiast can't also be expected to be an accomplished internist who knows the human body inside and out. But that is why we get physicals and other preventative care before we notice a problem—we recognize that we need an expert opinion and a voice of experience.

Think of a time in your life when you were doing something completely new and challenging—maybe your teenage years or your first serious relationship or parenting your first child. Whatever time you are thinking of, you can probably recall some decisions you made that were, if not outright mistakes, at least not optimum. You probably did the best you could with the information you had, but that information was necessarily incomplete because you'd never had that particular experience before.

For most of us, these bumps in the road are learning experiences that we can apply to situations later in life, and in the majority of cases, they don't lead to any disastrous outcomes. But imagine if you had a time machine and you could go back to one of those moments when you were muddling through without a guide and tell yourself everything you'd learned from years of trial and error. You'd probably make a few adjustments, right? Maybe a *lot* of adjustments.

Consider me your personal time machine. I am here to help you sidestep the many pitfalls of retirement—not just the ones that everyone fears but also the problems that most people don't even see coming.

CHAPTER TWO:

WHAT WILL YOU RETIRE TO?

The concept of retirement may *seem* like it has been around forever, but it's actually a pretty recent innovation. For much of human history, retirement as an organized social program simply didn't exist. Of course, people throughout history have stopped working because of age or disability, and people often took on different roles at different times in their lives, but there was no formalized system for when to do that or how to survive without regular income. Most people worked until they died because there wasn't really any other option.

Yes, there were cultural and religious traditions about children caring for their aged parents or semiformalized charity directed at those unable to work, but true retirement couldn't really exist without some type of widespread financial support system. Rome had a pension program, but only for soldiers, and while some cultures adopted the practice and even expanded pensions to include civil servants like firefighters or police, wide-scale retirement wasn't really feasible until the late nineteenth century.

Otto von Bismarck, Germany's chancellor in the late 1880s, created the first blanket pension program for everyone over sixty-five. Von Bismarck faced criticism over the decision, but he was convinced that allowing the disabled and elderly to leave the workforce without facing homelessness and starvation would boost the German economy. Otto von Bismarck was also what we would consider a conservative politician, and he was concerned by the widespread popularity of Marxist thought in Germany. He hoped that the pension idea would mollify some of his critics and put a stop to calls for more dramatic policy changes. His program was successful and popular and eventually became the model for other social welfare programs like Social Security here in the United States. America did lag behind Germany in terms of widespread retirement programs, though most major industries began offering pensions around the turn of the twentieth century.

It makes a certain kind of sense that it took us thousands of years to really develop a formalized system because, for a long time, we simply didn't live long enough to retire. Life expectancy statistics for the past can be a bit tricky because the comparison is often made between our life expectancy at birth (LEB), which is not always the most useful metric. Infant and child mortality rates were sky-high for most of human history—it was by far the most vulnerable period of our lives—and so many children died before reaching adulthood that it often skewed the data. For example, if you were a wealthy man in England in the 1400s, your LEB would be thirty, which seems extremely low (and on par with our stereotypes about life in the Dark Ages). If, however, you managed to survive to age twenty-one, your life expectancy was sixty-nine, which is not so far off from a modern American man's life expectancy.[3]

Still, humans really did live shorter lives for most of history, which meant that few working people reached the sixty-five or seventy age cutoff required of traditional retirement programs. The average life expectancy for a twenty-year-old American man at the time Otto von Bismarck rolled out his plan was still only about sixty-one. Even if someone did manage to make it to retirement age, they might only live to draw their pension for a few additional years. There were always outliers, of course, but retirement was conceived and designed as something to help people through the very end of their lives, not a state people could remain in for decades.

But the global forces that made retirement desirable and possible were also changing other things about how we lived. The Industrial Revolution, changes in social standards and state governance, advances in public health—all of these things contributed to an atmosphere in which, suddenly, people started living longer. A *lot* longer, in many cases. The current life expectancy for an American man of twenty is 77.3. If you do make it to 65, your average life expectancy is boosted to 84.5—and that's 86.7 for women. A quarter of 65-year-olds live to 90, and a tenth live to 100.[4]

Consider that: a system that was designed around the idea that, by age sixty-five, a person has contributed all they can to the workforce and will surely die soon is now being applied to a world where people remain healthy, vigorous, and alive well into their eighties. Surprisingly, very little about the concept has been adapted or changed since von Bismarck's day. Most significantly, we still think and talk about retire-

---

3   H. O. Lancaster, Expectations of Life: A Study in the Demography, Statistics and History of World Mortality (New York: Springer, 1990), 8.

4   Elizabeth Arias, Jiaquan Xiu, and Kenneth D. Kochanek, "United States Life Tables, 2016," National Vital Statistics Reports 68:4, May 7, 2019.

ment the same way we did at the turn of the last century. We often approach retirement as a finish line after which we can simply relax and be—and this was a fine way of looking at it when retirement lasted a handful of years at the very end of one's life. Now, some of us are spending twenty or thirty years in retirement—our retirements are old enough to vote, rent a car, and should probably start saving for their *own* retirements!

> Now, some of us are spending twenty or thirty years in retirement—our retirements are old enough to vote, rent a car, and should probably start saving for their own retirements!

Most people are not psychologically prepared for retirement because they simply aren't thinking about it in the right terms. It is a full phase of our lives at this point, and if you're going to be successful in it, you need to have a plan. Even people who have clearly thought about retirement in certain ways—people who have all the appropriate investments and financial structures in place—often have no long-range goals or ideas about how they will fill their time once they leave work behind.

Part of the problem is that, just as our health and life expectancy has changed dramatically in the last hundred years or so, the nature of work has changed as well. In 1890 a large proportion of work was, in one way or another, manual labor, often of the most physically punishing varieties. Even artisans relied upon a certain amount of physical strength and dexterity. As people aged and they absorbed injuries and illnesses, they became less and less able to do the kinds of work available to them. In modern America, white-collar and non-physical jobs are much more prevalent, meaning that people aren't necessarily retiring because they are no longer capable of doing their job. Instead, we retired because we are ready to move on from our jobs or, more commonly, because we've reached the arbitrary age when retirement is just what one does.

But no matter how attractive the idea might seem after a long, busy week, most people don't really want to be idle. In fact, there's a lot of evidence that having some sort of "work," whether it be a formal job, a hobby, or a social role like caring for children, keeps people healthier for longer. Our brains need to be exercised just like any other muscle, and when we stop challenging ourselves mentally, we can accelerate a slide into some forms of dementia, just as forgoing physical exercise exacerbates all sorts of illness. A lack of structure and meaningful occupation also increases rates of depression and anxiety, even substance abuse. The old saying about idle hands being the devil's workshop is true in many ways. Without things to do—things that engage and interest us and make us feel like we are contributing—we turn all our frustrated energy inward on ourselves and suffer.

We derive a lot of our self-worth from our work. For many of us, success and failure in our business has been the primary way of judging how well we are doing in life for a long time. If you spend thirty or forty years doing something and judging yourself by how well you do it, you are inevitably going to make that thing part of your identity as well. Think about when someone asks, "Who are you?" Your occupation is probably one of the first things you mention, after your name and maybe familial roles. What are we when we're no longer a CFO or a chemist or a financial advisor?

In addition to this rather existential question, the end of work often means big changes to our social lives. We may not always love our coworkers or bosses, but those interactions do make up a large percentage of the interpersonal interactions we have every day. Even ancillary social "relationships," like a nodding acquaintance with the barista at the coffee shop across from your office, add something to our lives, and when those relationships aren't available anymore, it can be disconcerting.

After the dust settles and people finish doing all the traveling they've wanted to do or finally take that painting class, they have to reckon with the lack of that social engagement and creative challenge. How do we transition from seeing dozens of people on a regular basis to not having to leave our houses all day if we don't feel like it? Without the structure, challenge, and engagement an occupation provides, it's very easy for a person to atrophy, both in their body and their minds.

The retirement period is also one of the more nebulous times in our lives, when we have the least amount of specific guidance about what to do with our time. We know generally what we're supposed to be doing as kids, and K–12 education provides a lot of structure for our lives. As young adults, we can safely expect to start our working lives or pursue higher education, and while that may look different for each individual, it's still a good general game plan. Retirement, however, is completely free-form. It's defined by what we *don't* do—we don't work anymore—but beyond that, anything goes.

When I ask my clients about their retirement plans, I get a lot of what I would consider "the fantasy of retirement." This is the image of retirement in popular culture with the happy former worker relaxing on a beach, mai tai in hand. Or a whirlwind trip to Paris. Or a leisurely golf game every day. To be clear, there's nothing wrong with looking forward to retirement or planning to enjoy oneself; the problem is one of scale. No matter how much you love travel or golf or even mai tais, a well-rounded life needs to include more than just leisure. You might be able to focus exclusively on relaxation for a few months or even years, but eventually, you are going to run into the law of diminishing returns. The most delicious food in the world loses its luster when you eat it three times a day, and even a beachfront paradise can become boring if there's nothing to do when you're there.

In my experience, people know what they want to do in retirement, but what very few have thought about is *what they need*. The key to a successful, fulfilling retirement is to create a structure (both financial and logistical) that balances those two interests . It's totally fine to say, "When I retire, I'm going to visit every continent," as long as you also have a plan for spending your time between and after those trips. How will you stay engaged and challenge yourself? How will you organize your days to create a predictable schedule? What will you do that fulfills you and makes you feel accomplished? How will you stay healthy, not just physically but mentally and socially?

That last question is one that I find people really struggle with in retirement. Most people aren't prepared for how their social life is going to change when they stop working. I've already mentioned the problem of the Incredible Shrinking Social Circle, but an arguably bigger issue is how relationships with our immediate family—particularly spouses—can change dramatically. People have a fantasy about engaging with their husbands and wives in retirement the same way they have fantasies about taking up golf or mountain climbing. They imagine that having more time with their spouse will inevitably mean a better, more loving relationship. Often, people even assume that any problems or issues they have in their marriage will be solved by having no work responsibilities and lots of free time to focus on the other person.

In reality, if you go from seeing someone mainly on nights and weekends to spending twenty-four hours a day with them, your relationship will change, and not always for the better. This is an especially important consideration for people who had especially demanding and time-intensive careers. These couples may go from having a few hours a week together to suddenly being joined at the hip all the time, and the whiplash from that change can be shocking.

No matter what configuration of retirements you have, it can introduce new stressors into your relationship. If you retire before your spouse, it's easy to feel abandoned and lonely, and that can lead to putting more pressure on your working spouse to spend their limited free time with you. It can even foment resentment if you begin to envy the time your partner spends working. If you are both retired, you may each be struggling with how to fill your days while also getting used to the simple friction of constantly sharing space with another person. One very common issue, especially given the generation that most current retirees belong to, is men retiring to wives who have worked in the home for most of the marriage. Suddenly, you have these creative, driven people who are looking for fulfillment in a sphere that has been managed and controlled by the other partner for decades. This can cause so much frustration for both parties and can, if not managed properly, really poison what should be a special time in a marriage.

Recent studies from the Pew Research Center found that retirees are the fastest-growing demographic for divorce—the divorce rate for people over fifty has doubled since 1990.[5] From what I've seen in my career, there is a definite correlation between an unconsidered retirement and marital strife. In the same way that people assume "living their dream" will fulfill all other needs, people don't make a plan for engaging with their spouse in retirement because they assume that love conquers all. Love and commitment are powerful, but they need some help from prudence and good planning as well. We have a client

---

5   Renee Stepler, "Led by Baby Boomers, Divorce Rates Climb
     for America's 50+ Population," Fact Tank, March 9, 2017,
     https://www.pewresearch.org/fact-tank/2017/03/09/
     led-by-baby-boomers-divorce-rates-climb-for-americas-50-population/.

who, just this month, got a part-time job, not for the money but just to get out the house a few days a week.

A few years ago, I had a client come in on her own, without her husband, to beg me to get him back to some sort of work. His job had had him traveling the world and spending long periods of time away from home for thirty years. In retirement, he was at a loss and basically followed his wife around all day. This state of affairs had his wife tearing out her hair, and I'm sure her husband wasn't exactly happy with how things were going either. He was used to waking up in a new city every week, and now the most exciting place he went was the local Starbucks.

Eventually, that client started participating in a mentoring program that got him out and engaged with others. Taking a little bit of the pressure off his wife, both to be his entire social network and keep him active and interested all day, did wonders for their relationship and the atmosphere in the house. My client was also much happier being able to do something useful for someone else.

Sometimes, when I raise this issue for folks—especially those who are approaching but have not yet reached retirement—I find that they have an almost allergic reaction to the idea of a "working retirement." Naturally, people want to take a break after a quarter century of dedicated labor, but what they don't necessarily understand is just how different "work" can be after retirement. Taking a part-time position with few responsibilities and lower stakes is a world apart from a grueling sixty-hour workweek. Money makes a huge difference in this as well. Voluntarily choosing to contribute to an industry or community you care about is completely different than feeling trapped in a job by mortgages and kids to feed. If you start something in retirement and decide it isn't working for you, you have the freedom to move on to something else, and even having that knowledge in the back of your head can reduce a lot of the stress and anxiety we often associate with work.

It doesn't have to be "work," either, let alone something in the same industry you left. Maybe you've always wanted to be a dog trainer or a scuba instructor or a painter—whatever you think will keep you active and engaged with the world. Retirement can be a time of tremendous personal growth and creative fulfillment; you can explore passions and interests you never had time to indulge before. Or you can park yourself in front of the TV ten hours a day. The choice is yours, but I know what I would recommend.

CHAPTER THREE:

DECISIONS, DECISIONS

There are as many ways to get down a mountain as there are mountains to climb—and people to climb them. Rappelling, down-climbing, "walking off"—a climber has an array of choices before them once they reach the peak, and no one solution is right for every situation. The decisions that an individual makes on top of a mountain rely heavily upon their ability to assess themselves, their circumstances, and the terrain before them as it exists at the beginning of the descent. That is a very important caveat, because the top of a mountain (whether literal or metaphorical) is not exactly the ideal place to make measured, thoughtful decisions.

If you've read or seen anything about climbing or specifically about Mount Everest in the past decade or two, you've probably heard of the 1996 disaster on Everest, detailed in outdoor writer John Krakauer's book *Into Thin Air*. That book and the flurry of additional narratives, articles, TV specials, and even Hollywood films about the tragedy have been obsessed with trying to dissect and understand why people made the choices they made that day at the summit. In particular, most conversations around the event focus on Rob Hall and Scott Fischer, leaders of the two "adventure guide" companies that were helping larger parties get up the mountain and, ideally, back down again safely. Both men were extremely experienced, both as climbers in their own right and as guides for others.

Yet on that day in 1996, both men made choices that put themselves and their clients in danger. Perhaps no single choice was more disastrous than the decision both leaders made to allow their clients to keep trying for the summit long after the cutoff time they had established at base camp. That time limit was put in place to make sure that nobody ended up descending the mountain in the dark, but it took on even more dire significance when overshooting the limit also put them right in the path of an unexpectedly brutal blizzard that evening.

Hall and Fischer couldn't have anticipated a sudden blizzard, just like they couldn't have anticipated the unusual number of people on the mountain that day and the bottlenecks that ensued. Others have suggested that the clients' intense desire to get to the top ("summit fever," as it is often called) may have softened the guides' resolve. The biggest confounding factor, however, had to be the physiological effect that the high altitude had on everyone climbing that day. Altitude sickness can begin at 8,000 feet above sea level, and Mount Everest's base camp (where climbers rest and acclimatize before attempting the summit) is at 17,600 feet. The summit itself is approximately 29,000 feet above sea level, and the human body is simply not designed to spend long periods of time at such elevations. Oxygen deprivation to that extreme can quickly inhibit brain function.

Tragically, Hall and Fisher were acutely aware of this problem. According to Rob Hall's widow, he even had a rule that climbers shouldn't make decisions at high altitude because the atmosphere (literal and metaphorical) was just too obfuscating. The problem is that, no matter how meticulously and completely you make your plan on flat ground, you are always going to have to adapt by the time you reach the peak. That's because the trip up the mountain changes everything: it changes your physical condition and energy level and your supplies, and even the mountain itself can change between the base and the summit.

It doesn't feel entirely fair that we should have to make critical decisions in those moments when we are most vulnerable to the intense stressors all around us, but that is also the place where we have the most complete, up-to-the minute information about our situation. Is a storm approaching? How much oxygen do we have? Are there climbers below us? How soon until darkness falls? All of these are questions that we can't really answer until we are preparing to make our descent.

So what can we do if we have to make decisions at these intense moments when there's so much riding on each choice and we ourselves may not have the clearest idea of how to proceed? We can consult someone else, a neutral party with specialized knowledge who is not under the same stresses and limitations. A significant component of the 1996 disaster was the fact that guides in that case were subject to the same disorienting and depleting effects of high altitude and exhaustion as everyone else.

When it comes to Mount Retirement, my job is to stay at sea level and keep a clear head. That means that the most important thing I can get from a client early on is the view from their personal summit. The information you provide and the goals you describe allow me to set a course and get you where you want to be . With that course in mind, I can advise you as you make those critical choices about how you personally plan to get back on solid ground.

Just like on an actual mountain, there are numerous ways to tackle retirement, and despite what the common wisdom might say about this type of savings vehicle or that style of investment, there is no one-size-fits-all approach. With that in mind, there are still some nearly universal factors at work, and below I've assembled a basic list of the major types of decisions you will probably need to make as you approach your own summit.

1. DECIDE ON A TIMELINE THAT WORKS.

A lot of people approach retirement somewhat passively. They plan to leave their job, not necessarily when it would be most beneficial but whenever it is customary (or mandatory). Similarly, people often assume that if they follow general recommendations in terms of savings vehicles and amounts to set aside each year, they will automatically accrue enough wealth to retire by the time they are ready to do so. People also need to decide when and how to do things like draw a pension or file for Social Security, and they will often default to the "norm" (usually the earliest possible option) rather than finding a personalized solution.

The problem with general solutions is twofold: they *mostly* work in *most* cases. If you deviate from the norm—or just happen to be unlucky—you'll wind up with a plan that is, at best, underserving you and that, at worst, won't actually cover your expenses in retirement. Almost everyone benefits from actually running the numbers and seeing how far their current savings will go with their projected yearly expenses. To do this effectively, you have to ...

2. DECIDE HOW YOU WILL SPEND YOUR TIME IN RETIREMENT.

We talked a bit about this concept in the previous chapter, but this is the part where we get a bit more granular about filling our days. I want my clients to have a clear, workable plan for budgeting their time so I can budget their income to match. If you are planning to travel, to golf, or even just to spend time with your grandkids, I still need to know the logistics of these choices. How many weeks per year will you allocate to travel? How often will you purchase new golfing equipment or pay club membership fees? Will you make any modifications to or remodel your home? The more fleshed out and specific your plans, the more precise and helpful I can be as we…

3. DECIDE ON A BUDGET.

Budgeting effectively for retirement is a skill that many people take for granted. Often, clients don't think much about this element of retiring because they believe they already know how to budget—after all, they've been doing it their entire working lives. When you're in the accumulation stage, however, you are managing an inflow and an outflow, and in the disbursement stage, that's almost reversed. You suddenly have a finite amount of wealth with a limited ability to accrue more, and you have to manage the outflow without depleting your asset base too quickly. If someone is unprepared for this change, all of their planning and instincts can actually work against them.

It's my job to help people shift those gears and learn to think differently about income and expenses. I often liken the experience to going to a country where everyone drives on the left side of the road. If you're prepared (and maybe practice a little), you can get the hang of it pretty quickly. But if you were somehow dropped into that situation unexpectedly, you'd total your car in minutes.

Not only is the retirement phase very different from a financial perspective, it's also a distinct—and unique—phase of life. The way you spend money is going to change as you age, and I find that people often fail to account for that in their budgets. For example, a client might tell me they like to travel, so they want to build a $10,000 travel budget into their overall plan. That's fine and perfectly doable, but I probably don't need to keep that component in the budget indefinitely. Most people aren't planning on sprinting up Machu Picchu when they're 104.

Whenever I dig into these items, I am usually able to create something more customized that gives the client greater flexibility and even opens up other avenues for spending their time and cash. Maybe they really only want to do a world tour right when they retire, so after those first five years, we can scale that part of the plan back and reallocate those resources. Maybe they want to gradually step down their travel spending over the course of fifteen or twenty years.

In general, most people significantly reduce their spending around age eighty. No matter what kind of life you lead, most people naturally settle into a more conservative lifestyle with less travel and fewer new purchases as they age. Even the medical expenses that people assume will inflate their spending in those years are generally cut significantly by Medicare. Many people entering retirement incorrectly assume that their spending will be static—or even increase due to inflation—for the rest of their lives. The biggest impact this has on planning is a needless restriction of resources in early retirement, which is, ironically, the time when most people are best able to make good use of that money.

Having more income available in the earlier stages of retirement when you are healthiest and most active just makes sense. Yet many financial planners and sometimes clients themselves structure their budgets so austerely, all for imagined expenses that almost certainly aren't going to happen. There's something to be said for saving for a rainy day, but this is more like spending your whole paycheck on umbrellas when you live in the Sahara.

Sometimes, this is an extension of a lifetime habit of saving instead of spending. Many people come to me having carefully squirreled away money for years with the goal of making it through retirement. Once the time actually comes to spend that money on the business of being retired, however, it's hard to let those carefully honed instincts go. For those clients, I generally ask them what they are actually going to do with that money they've allocated when they are eighty-seven or ninety. Most don't have a concrete answer because it's often a choice made more out of emotion than practical need. Specifically, people are often afraid of running out of income before they run out of years. Our plans ensure that won't happen because we …

4. DECIDE HOW YOU WILL MITIGATE YOUR RISKS IN RETIREMENT.

Unless you've worked with a financial planner specifically focused on retirement, the odds are good that some elements of your financial portfolio are not going to be ideally situated for the journey ahead. The biggest issue is usually that, just as people are psychologically still in an accumulation mindset, their portfolios are also organized for accumulation.

A portfolio designed to gather and grow assets is fundamentally different than one designed to disburse those assets, and the main difference is the approach to something called the sequence-of-returns risk. We touched on this idea earlier—in the accumulation phase, it's the average growth rate that matters for any investment product, whereas once you enter the disbursement phase, the timing of returns becomes critical. Many people underestimate or miss this risk entirely. It's very easy to look at an investment, see a 6 percent average growth and think, "OK, so I'll draw 5 percent every year and still have that 1 percent annual growth." In actuality, that 6 percent average is years of +11 and -8 balancing one another out, and, in a bad year, taking 5 percent out of an investment could mean drawing a much bigger chunk of your asset base than you'd planned.

The market is inherently unpredictable, a bit like extreme weather. If you happen to build your house in the wrong place at the wrong time, a tornado or a hurricane could touch down one day and destroy everything you've worked so hard to establish. But the thing about both bad weather and market risks is that we are constantly developing new and better ways to insulate people from their effects. There is an array of products and strategies we can use to protect your wealth and avoid the domino effect that comes from taking too much out of an investment at the wrong time.

The key to protecting yourself is to find the right products and …

5. DECIDE HOW TO STRUCTURE YOUR PORTFOLIO.

At the most basic level, the solution to market risk is the same as the solution to many other types of risk: diversification—or the "Don't put your eggs in one basket" principle, as your grandparents might have called it. You've probably heard that having a diverse portfolio is important and that you should change the nature of that diversity as you move through different parts of your life, and that's still generally true. What has changed—and is constantly changing—is the specific products that are best suited to various scenarios. The conditions of the market and the general economy

> Almost any blanket statement about a specific product being "good" or "bad" is pretty useless in reality.

are constantly adjusting the value and utility of different savings vehicles, while new laws and investment options are even changing the nature of the products themselves. There's a lot of common wisdom about which products to buy when for maximum benefit, but the problem is, by the time things become common wisdom, conditions have already shifted.

Even professional financial advisors don't always have the best or most current information, unless they pay a lot of attention to products designed for retirement. That is why we developed a company that is focused primarily on retirement, because so often, traditional planners overlook a lot of detail and nuance about retirement issues. Annuities are a great example of this problem. I'll expand more on them in their own chapter, but suffice it to say that annuities are more complicated—and more useful—than the somewhat negative reputation they have had throughout their history would suggest.

Almost any blanket statement about a specific product being "good" or "bad" is pretty useless in reality. That's because there's actually a lot of important diversity, not just in the different types of products we can use in retirement, but even within the products themselves. Annuity A might be nothing like Annuity B, and while perhaps A would be a disaster for your portfolio, B might be a great fit for a portion of your portfolio. It's my job to know all about Annuities A and B and be able to present all your options, not just the most widely used or most traditional. This kind of specialized knowledge is exactly why people hire experienced guides in the first place.

There's been a lot of interesting research recently into the science of decision-making. One of the most compelling trends scientists have discovered is the very significant role emotion plays in the process. It seems, in fact, that while we may think of ourselves as rational creatures, we often use logic and reason primarily to justify the choices we've already made out of emotion. This process happens so fast that we don't even realize exactly what we're doing. Whenever there's a seemingly senseless tragedy like the '96 Everest disaster, we always go searching for the logic in people's actions—and inactions—but the truth is that we can't ever know why someone else makes a choice and, perhaps, neither can they. No decision is ever free from emotion, but we can get closer to a neutral weighing of options with two important tools: more information and outside input. When you partner with a good advisor and give them usable data, suddenly that opaque path ahead of us becomes clear: it's just a series of simple steps, all the way home.

CHAPTER FOUR:

CREATING A TAX PLAN

When it comes to topics we often tackle more emotionally than logically, perhaps none is more significant than taxes. It may sound like a contradiction at first—taxes are a pretty dry subject; who gets emotional over spreadsheets and income brackets? As it turns out, a lot of us. Maybe we aren't weeping over columns of numbers, but when you ask the average person what they believe or even "know" about their taxes, you'll get a lot more subjective impressions than empirical facts.

If I asked a roomful of people whether they felt like they were paying "a lot" in taxes—and I have—I'd probably get a small range of response but, in general, most people would report feeling like they did indeed pay "a lot." If I tweaked the question just a bit and asked them if they felt they paid *enough* in taxes, I'd get a bit more diversity in responses, depending on each person's individual situation and their perspectives on the economy as a whole. "A lot" and "enough" are both subjective terms, however. Many of my clients might have a quarterly tax bill that amounts to more than someone's yearly income, after all.

So I also ask them if they feel that people generally are paying more or less in taxes than earlier points in American history, and it's that question that really shows how much emotion, nostalgia, memory, and perception can shape our understanding of "the facts."

That question (whether we are currently in a high or low personal income tax rate environment, relative to history) has a correct answer, but you'd be surprised how few of us know it. For most of us, historical comparisons are very personal and gut driven. People often assume personal income tax is currently high, sometimes even unusually or historically high, relative to the past because of how they felt in the past. If they grew up in an economically comfortable family or they themselves were successful and didn't feel an undue tax burden, they believe that those things must have been correlated with lower taxes on the individual. In reality, there are a great many factors that go into the discrepancy people are seeing between their memories and their current reality. Some of it is due to genuine economic changes that have made things like single-income families, for example, less common, but nostalgia also plays a big role. We are primed to remember our youth and childhood as carefree, and for most people, our parents would have actively shielded us from any economic woes they did have. When it comes to a past that we weren't even around for, our beliefs about what "things back then" were like are even less reliable.

So in the interest of having clear data, here's a chart showing the personal income tax rates from the turn of the last century to today:

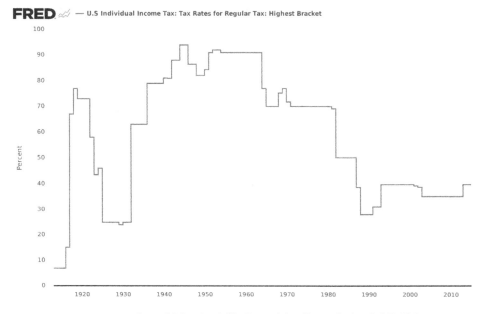

Source: U.S. Department of the Treasury, Internal Revenue Service   fred.stlouisfed.org

As you can see, we are actually in a dramatically lower personal tax environment than our parents and grandparents faced. In fact, around the end of World War II (a time that many think of when they imagine an especially prosperous time in America), the personal tax rate reached its zenith at 94 percent.[6] All of this is more than just interesting trivia, however. It is vitally important data that helps us do one of the hardest things we have to do with our retirement plans: predict the future.

Every plan is, to some degree, an attempt to guess what will happen in the future and prepare accordingly, but for retirement plans, this kind of educated guessing is especially critical. Our adaptability is limited in retirement, as we are managing finite resources, often to

6   Historical Highest Marginal Income Tax Rates. (January 19, 2019). Retrieved from https://www.taxpolicycenter.org/statistics/ historical-highest-marginal-income-tax-rates.

their exhaustion. If the future surprises you at the wrong time, you may not have the flexibility or asset base to work around that surprise. That's why it's always best to do as much research and to gather as much information as possible before we start strategizing.

Of course, as Mark Twain allegedly said, history doesn't repeat itself, but it often rhymes. Knowing what has happened in the past is not going to give us a perfect image of the future, but it does give us information about trends, circumstances, and behaviors that we might see again. So what does this specific history of the tax rate in America tell us about its future? Well, for one thing, it tells us that we are on the very low end of the spectrum currently and don't have a lot of room to move further in that direction. Taxes can—and have—gone much higher, often during times of national strife, like wars or economic depressions. This suggests to me that, one way or another, the pendulum will probably swing back. Either we are going to hit the lower limit on personal taxes, or a major event is going to force a change, but the current trajectory is probably not going to continue unimpeded.

A good prognosticator looks at more than just historical data, however. I also monitor current events and changes going on in the world and the country right now when I am making predictions about how tax law might look in the future. And the thing about the current tax situation is that it is untenable. Whether you are a Democrat or a Republican or somewhere in between, we all have to agree that the government likes to spend money, and it's been spending a whole lot of it for a long time. We are currently running a $20 trillion deficit, and that cannot be sustained forever. In fact, in the time between the first draft of this book and the final edit, it swelled to *$22 trillion*! When a country needs money—as America surely will—it gets it largely by taxing its people, especially people in a certain income bracket.

This is another point where people often have a misperception about taxes. When I ask my room full of people who pays the majority of the nation's tax bill, almost everyone in there says something like "the middle class." That's a very common mistake, probably because changes in taxes are often framed in terms of their impact upon the middle and working classes. While even small increases or decreases in tax rates can have a huge impact upon the lives of families of modest means, the reality is that only about 20 percent of the money generated by income taxes actually comes from those families.

Approximately 87 percent of the revenue raised by individual income taxes comes from the wealthiest 20 percent of Americans, and the figures only get steeper the higher up the socioeconomic ladder you go. The literal top 1 percent of the country paid about 43 percent of the total tax bill in 2018 (for reference, the 1 percent comprises approximately one million households). Why is this? Well, for one thing, the "middle class" is smaller than it used to be—about 10 percent smaller on average than it was in 1971—and the true "upper class" has also shrunk, consolidating a lot of wealth into a relatively narrow slice of the population.[7]

Personal income tax is designed to increase as one's income goes up, under the assumption that those who have more can contribute more without experiencing financial hardship. Also, the government is certainly canny enough to figure out where the money is and to go after it. The middle and working classes simply aren't the revenue generators that the top 20 percent are. Again, I'm not making any political, social, or moral conclusions about this information. Whatever you believe personally about this system is your own business; my job is

---

7   "The American Middle Class Is Losing Ground," Pew Research Center: Social and Demographic Trends, December 9, 2015, https://www.pewsocialtrends. org/2015/12/09/the-american-middle-class-is-losing-ground/.

to understand how it works and help my clients navigate it and meet their goals within it.

In summary, the country is going to need money in the future; it is probably going to get that money from people with larger incomes and more wealth; to that end, taxes will likely be changed and increased. That is my general prediction for the future, and I use that framework to start developing tax plans for my clients. I also presume that, generally speaking, my clients want to avoid paying more than they have to in taxes. It might seem like I wouldn't even have to specify that last part, but it's surprising how nonintuitive some tax reduction strategies can be and how even people who are actively trying to protect their wealth can wind up in situations where they've needlessly put themselves at risk.

> It's surprising how nonintuitive some tax reduction strategies can be and how even people who are actively trying to protect their wealth can wind up in situations where they've needlessly put themselves at risk.

Possibly the best example is that of funding retirement plans. Almost everyone who has done any retirement savings at all has a 401(k), likely a traditional 401(k)—at this point, 401(k)s are practically synonymous with "retirement savings" in general. Most of my clients opened a 401(k) because someone at some point told them it was a good way to save for their future, and then my clients simply put the appropriate amount of money in each year and didn't think much more about it until they were actually facing the prospect of retirement.

The traditional 401(k) does have a lot of benefits, chief among them that contributions toward it are tax deductible, which means you can essentially invest a chunk of your income tax free. Another theoretically valuable feature is the way 401(k) offers "tax deferral," meaning that the money is only taxed when you withdraw it in the future, not as it grows. When you fund your 401(k) or when the money in that 401(k) grows via investments, that income is essentially invisible as far as your tax return is concerned for that year. This means you could reduce your overall taxable income in a given tax year while still keeping that money for your future use.

At least, that's how it's supposed to work in theory. The value of these provisions depends on a few important presumptions—mainly that you will be in a lower income tax bracket during retirement than during your working life and that the tax rate will be similar or even more favorable at that time. You can probably already see some potential problems with this arrangement. Imagine patiently "deferring" your income during years of 26 percent or 27 percent personal income tax rates, only to start withdrawing it after the rate has gone up to 40 percent or 50 percent. While compounded tax-deferred growth made your account bigger, now it is under a tax attack.

The other major flaw with the traditional 401(k) is that it does not give you the option to leave your money for as long as you want. Seventy-two is the magical age for most people when they have to start withdrawing a certain amount of money from their 401(k)/IRA or be faced with a penalty. This can put people in the untenable position of having to withdraw money they may not need, thus increasing their income and subsequently their tax rate. Not making the distributions isn't really a viable option, either, because the fine is 50 percent of the mandatory withdrawal—likely even worse than the bite taxes would have taken.

As I touched on before when we talked about the sequence-of-returns risk, timing is critical in retirement. It's not just about the money itself but also about when the money comes, and even small changes can make a huge difference. For example, under the current tax system, a married couple can have income of roughly $112,000 and pay an effective federal tax rate of about 15 percent. These figures are for a couple, however—everything is halved for a single person. Now, in retirement it's very common—some might even say inevitable—for a household to go from being taxed as a couple to being taxed as an individual, and that is where the problems begin.

When you pass away, your assets typically pass to your spouse, and if your spouse is old enough, those funds will be subject to the required minimum distribution rules. This means that your spouse could very abruptly find themselves bumped up into a higher tax bracket, Additionally, as you get older, the percent of your account that must be distributed for RMDs gets bigger each year. This can have a trickle-down effect and impact what it costs you to pay for Medicare as well as limit certain itemized deductions. which has implications for more than just your tax bill.

These aren't necessarily fatal flaws; no investment vehicle is perfect, and for many people, the benefits of the traditional 401(k) can outweigh its drawbacks. The ubiquity of the traditional 401(k) has gotten people to think of it as an almost mandatory part of the retirement portfolio. Most people assume that because it is so standard, it has to be the best general option, and that perception is only bolstered by the fact that most employers offer 401(k)s. It all comes back to the fundamental issue of not knowing what we don't know. If a person simply ticks all the retirement boxes, doing everything they are "supposed" to do, they could nevertheless miss out on any number of opportunities simply because they don't realize how much is actually available to them.

An additional problem with retirement savings is the constant march of time and innovation. The original IRA was introduced in 1975 and the traditional 401(k) in 1978, so there were lots of people for whom these were their only choices. I strongly prefer a Roth 401(k) or a Roth IRA for most situations, but the Roth didn't even exist until 1997. A person can hardly be blamed for not choosing an option that wasn't on the table, and people who don't work in the financial industry wouldn't necessarily have kept close tabs on every new type of retirement account to hit the market—especially when, as far as you know, you already have a perfectly good savings vehicle for your own retirement.

By this point, the existence of the Roth itself is well established, but there's still a lack of general awareness about the upsides of the Roth when compared with the traditional, which means that the Roth is really underutilized. The main difference between Roth and traditional 401(k)s or IRAs is how they each manage taxation—the structure is nearly reversed, in fact. Money you put into a Roth has already been taxed just like any other income, and it is when you start the disbursement process that you get to withdraw the money tax free. This already avoids one of the biggest issues with 401(k) taxation: the potential that you'll wind up withdrawing taxable money at a higher tax rate in retirement, but the benefits go further than that.

The Roth is more flexible when it comes to the terms of withdrawal. You are not required to take disbursements at a specific time, leaving you free to keep growing those savings if you don't need the additional income. This, plus the tax-free disbursement, is a large part of what makes the Roth a really great vehicle for legacy savings. If you want to pass money to your children or other heirs without also handing them a huge tax bill, the Roth, while not the only way, is a great way to do that. Finally, unlike the traditional option, the Roth

IRA allows you to keep funding the account for as long as you'd like. The traditional IRA requires you to stop contributing money when you start the disbursement phase at seventy-two. Not only is this great for bequests and inheritances, but it's also helpful for people who started saving for retirement later in life. If you came to me at the age of sixty or so and wanted to save for retirement, it wouldn't make much sense to simply open a traditional IRA that you could only fund for another twelve years. The Roth gives you a little more time in case you choose to work longer or simply want the extra security of continuing to save.

The Roth IRA versus the traditional offers a kind of classic delayed gratification dilemma: Do you take the tax-free money now or wait for the future? This plays on our impulsivity as well as our uncertainty—it's very tempting to immediately grab a benefit or reward, especially when you don't know whether it will still be available in the future. It is possible that your tax rate could decline in retirement (in fact, this is the traditional wisdom, as most retired people are expected to be in a lower tax bracket than those actively working) or that you could not live long enough to take enough tax-free withdrawals to balance out the years of taxed deposits. The Roth also does have some drawbacks. People with incomes over a certain threshold may not be eligible to open one (though there are some ways to work around that restriction). Also, Roth payments won't reduce your total taxable income the way traditional IRA payments will.

> The real problem is that most people aren't allocating their money as strategically as possible, especially when it comes to preparing for taxation.

Fortunately, there's no reason a person can't have a Roth and a traditional IRA (among any number of other investments). The choice isn't really which account to have; it's how to fund those accounts to get the maximum benefit. The real problem is that most people aren't allocating their money as strategically as possible, especially when it comes to preparing for taxation, and the underutilization of Roth IRAs is the just most common manifestation of that problem that I see.

The financial management industry has an unfortunate blind spot when it comes to taxes, mainly because a lot of people get their financial advice in a piecemeal fashion. They might have one person for general financial advice, another person for retirement planning, and someone else to actually prepare their tax return. Each of these people may be great at their job, but as long as each one is only focusing on the area they were hired to manage, none of them are really considering the bigger picture. This is especially apparent when it comes to taxes because people so often make the mistake of not discerning between tax planners and tax preparers. Tax preparers are more common by far, and they range from the guy manning the desk at H&R Block to boutique personal accountants, but the thing they all have in common is that their job is to complete your tax return correctly. It is not their job to evaluate someone's finances and make changes or suggestions to save them money on taxes in the future. Some may indeed be very knowledgeable and able to help in this area, but it is not the norm. A tax preparer can be extremely good at their job while still being completely useless in terms of actually helping you avoid mistakes or protect your assets.

A perfect example happened to me recently when I met with a new client to review the tax returns he'd given me. I ask all my new clients to bring in their last few years of tax returns so I can get a fuller sense of their financial situation, and it's very common during this process to find places where things could be changed or improved. In the case of this particular client, he had been carrying forward a big net operating loss and wasn't really doing anything with it. Additionally, he had a well-funded traditional IRA but no Roth, and at that point in his life, his income was too high to contribute to a Roth. The thing is, while he couldn't put money into a Roth, he could still convert an account (specifically his traditional IRA) into a Roth. This practice has a number of benefits, but it's especially advantageous when utilizing net operating losses, because when you convert your traditional IRA into a Roth, you have to pay taxes on that money, just as you would have to if you were taking disbursements in retirement. When you have a big net-operating-loss carryforward, however, you can apply that to your tax bill and thus eliminate or significantly reduce the rate of taxes you would have to pay on that conversion.

"Has your tax person ever talked to you about a loss conversion?" I asked him almost as soon as we sat down together.

"No," my client said. "What's a loss conversion?"

It's completely normal for the average client not to know what a loss conversion is. Unless they've already done one themselves, they'd really have no reason to learn about it, but my client seemed increasingly disturbed as I explained the process and how it could benefit him. "Conservatively speaking, you could probably convert about $200,000. If you want to be more aggressive, you could go up to $250,000."

"And that's tax free?"

"Well, it is taxed but, after we apply your operating losses, you'd zero out."

"And that money just stays in the Roth?"

"Yup, you can keep it there as long as you need or want, and it just keeps growing tax free."

He seemed a little stunned but very enthusiastic, and after a more careful review of all his finances, we settled on doing something in the middle with a net tax result of $0. He now has a robust Roth IRA that will continue to accrue value until he decides to start withdrawing money—money he will never pay taxes on again.

While we were in the middle of this process, however, he asked me an interesting question: "Why do you think my accountant never talked to me about this? It seems like such a good idea." It was a good idea, and for someone looking for ways to optimize his tax benefits, it was obvious. For someone who was simply focused on making sure that his return was prepared fully and accurately, however, it was a totally unnecessary extra step. The average tax preparer in America does between fifteen hundred and three thousand tax returns every year, and those are almost all done during "tax season"—just a few months in the spring. Tax preparers simply don't have time to comb through everyone's returns for opportunities or omissions.

"I don't know exactly why they didn't suggest this. Maybe they're not really tax planners, and they were more focused on the return itself?"

The lack of true holistic financial planning is endemic in the financial industry. Too many people presume that if someone is a good general accountant, they

> That is why Watermark Wealth Strategies consciously built a team packed with people who have specific expertise in addition to our training in retirement planning.

will be a good financial planner or a good tax preparer or a good tax strategist—or any permutation of those very different roles. In reality, most people have limits on their ability to specialize, and it's simply human nature to overlook things. This is especially true when we don't have enough knowledge to necessarily know when we're making a mistake or passing up an opportunity.

That is why Watermark Wealth Strategies consciously built a team packed with people who have specific expertise in addition to our training in retirement planning. In my case, I am as much a "tax guy" as I am a "retirement guy"—I got my master's degree in taxation and accounting, and I've been a CPA for more than twenty years now. I also work with other professionals with similar expertise, and we examine a client's financial portfolio from all perspectives to make sure we aren't missing something.

What you don't know can hurt you, actually. You just might not realize how you've been hurt until much later, if ever. Maybe my client never would have known that he could have converted, and maybe it wouldn't have made the difference between life and death for him, but would it have made the difference between tax brackets? Between lifestyles? Between leaving something behind for his heirs and leaving nothing? Fortunately, due to our comprehensive approach and tax-conscious strategy, he will never have to find out.

CHAPTER FIVE:

GETTING THE MOST FROM SOCIAL SECURITY

The one upside to the high-stakes complexity of taxes is that, generally speaking, people are aware of the risks involved and take steps to avoid them. Not everyone knows all the specific problems and pitfalls, but most people recognize that screwing up their taxes is both dangerous and dispiritingly easy to do. That's why we have a tax-preparation industry, after all. When it comes to other aspects of our financial health, however, there's much less general awareness about the importance—and difficulty—of "getting it right." This is especially true of Social Security, which is, in many ways, even more of a potential trap for the unwary than taxes.

As frustrating and difficult as taxes can be, filing for Social Security is even more complex and less intuitive. There are over five hundred ways to claim Social Security and more than twenty-seven hundred rules about how to go through that process, many of them interrelated with the others. For example, here is the formula used to calculate benefits:

$$B(a) = PIA(a) \times (1-e(n)) \times (1 + d(n)) \times Z(a) + \max((.5 \times PIA^*(a) - PIA(a) \times (1+d(n)))) \times E(a), 0) \times (1- u(a,q,n,m)) \times D(a)^8$$

If you just recalled that recurring nightmare you have about showing up to an algebra test you didn't study for, don't worry: you are not alone. Social Security is not designed to be managed by the layman, yet that's overwhelmingly how it's been framed. People who wouldn't dream of doing their own taxes are fine trying to solo-navigate the alphabet soup you see above, all because filing is generally presented as a simple matter of paperwork, like getting a birth certificate or marriage license.

Additionally, the long-term, annual nature of taxation means that even if you do make a mistake, you'll usually have a chance to correct it in the future. Like the client I mentioned in the last chapter, you have the opportunity to learn from past returns and even course correct as your circumstances or goals shift. By contrast, you will only ever file for Social Security once in your life, and there's virtually no recourse if you do miss something.

Similarly, there's no industry around Social Security that offers professional help for filing. Sure, you might get the occasional pamphlet or workshop, but it's hardly common to have a "Social Security guy" the way many people have a "tax guy." Most people filing for SS are like a little white mouse dropped into the heart of an intricate maze—you have no idea where to go and no signposts to help you

---

8   Laurence J. Kotlikoff, Philip Moeller, and Paul Solman, Get   What's Yours: The Secrets to Maxing Out Your Social Security (New York: Simon & Schuster, 2015), 299.

get there. The mouse is even in a slightly better position: at least he can use his nose to find the cheese at the end of the maze. Most of us humans simply wind up making choices at random, with no way of knowing whether we've guessed correctly or, often, even what the difference between the two options was. A big part of the problem is how relatively hands-off the Social Security Administration is when it comes to optimizing your filing.

There's a joke I like to tell clients to explain the difference between the IRS and the Social Security Administration:

A husband and wife are stranded on a desert island with zero supplies and no sign of rescue on the horizon. Suddenly, the wife turns to the husband and asks, "Did you remember to pay the credit card bill before we left?"

The husband is a little nonplussed, but he answers, "No, I didn't."

"How about the mortgage payment?"

"No … "

"And the quarterly tax bill?"

"Nope."

To his surprise, the wife flops down on the sand and stretches out her feet comfortably. "Oh, good, then someone from the IRS should be coming to get us any minute now."

For better or for worse, if you are incorrectly filing your taxes (or failing to file them altogether), that situation is not going to go unaddressed for long. There's a certain failsafe with taxes that just isn't there with Social Security. If you think about it, the reason is clear: if you make one of the most common tax mistakes (and certainly if you fail to file), the IRS will probably lose money. If you fail to file for your Social Security or make a major mistake, the SSA usually gets to keep money.

That is possibly the biggest reason filing for Social Security is so much riskier than other elements of financial bureaucracy: no one is going to warn you or even alert you afterward if you screw something up. The SSA is actively prohibited from helping people optimize their filing beyond offering the basic FAQ-type answers about the process. Social Security as a program is in constant danger of being underfunded and becoming unsustainable; if everyone filed perfectly and got the maximum amount, the

> There is no one sitting at the SSA right now poring over a register to see who is eligible to file but hasn't done so yet.

problem would be even worse. As I like to tell clients, there is no one sitting at the SSA right now poring over a register to see who is eligible to file but hasn't done so yet. There is no one in charge of calling up Bill and Sally Smith and telling them they are giving up money every month—that is a job that does not exist.

And people do miss their deadlines; it's probably one of the most common mistakes I see people make with regard to Social Security. Just this month, I had to tell a new client that he needed to file immediately because he had been just leaving about $400 per month on the table for years at that point. Unfortunately, there was no way to recoup that money—the only thing we could do was stop the bleeding as soon as possible. There was no reason he had to lose that extra income, and while $400 may not seem like the biggest chunk of change, I've rarely met a client who wasn't interested in getting and keeping all of their Social Security benefits. Oddly enough, it's often my wealthiest clients who are the most adamant about making sure they get their full benefit. Maybe it's because they've spent years paying into the program, and that's created a sense of expectation, or maybe they are just the sort of person who would never waste or pass up money. I imagine that's a trait that might help someone become wealthy, in fact. You've probably read some of those calculations that indicate people like Warren Buffett would actually lose money if they took time out of their day to pick a twenty up off the street, but I can't imagine he'd be in the position he's in now if he were the type to ignore an opportunity to increase his wealth, even if only by $20.

On the other side of the coin (or bill …) there are people who are blithely hurtling toward sixty-two, assuming that they can file for Social Security when, in fact, they don't qualify. That's an especially big misconception that I run into fairly frequently: people believe that if they worked at all, they will get some degree of benefit from the SSA. In fact, you have to reach a certain threshold to make a claim : forty "credits," or forty working quarters, which works out to about ten years. Within each of those quarters, you have to earn at least $1,410 for it to count toward your forty-credit goal. This rule also has some caveats, depending on when you were born, any disabilities you may have, and work done within certain industries or tax-exempt groups. There are also some jobs that actually don't participate in Social Security, including certain civil-servant positions, so any time spent working in those positions will not help you accrue credits.

I find that this is mainly a challenge for women, who often spent a lot of their working lives in a more traditional domestic sphere. They may have spent a couple of decades as stay-at-home parents and only joined the workforce later in life or worked primarily in volunteer or other nonqualifying capacities. Just last month, I was working with a client who had done most of her work in a family business. It was an informal, volunteer-type arrangement, and the business was generally successful enough that she didn't have to seek much paying work elsewhere. Unfortunately, this left her with only thirty-eight eligible credits as she approached age sixty. She was so close to that forty mark but, in her case, there was no such thing as half credit; if she didn't make forty credits, she didn't get anything.

"Would it be possible for you to do some more work for the family business?" I asked her. "Compensated work, I mean. If you could earn $3,500 in one quarter, that would earn you those two additional credits."

"Sure," she said, seeming surprised it was that easy. "But won't I be taxed on that additional income?"

"You will. But if you keep it to just the $3,500 you need, you can secure yourself about $9,800 in additional income each year through Social Security, which should more than make up for it."

Because she came to me relatively early, she'll be able to make that simple change and, at sixty-two, she can start receiving a benefit for the rest of her life. If she hadn't learned about the forty-credits rule, she might have missed her chance—all because of a $3,500 gap in income.

Similarly, I had another client who had two solid pensions but didn't qualify for Social Security because of the type of work he'd done. The pensions were part of an overall package intended to replace Social Security, and my client had always assumed he didn't really need to file on top of his existing retirement benefits. However, he had married a woman from a different country relatively late in life, and her entire work history was outside the United States. There was no way she was going to qualify in time, but when I met them, the husband was just four credits short.

"Listen," I said, "I know it doesn't seem like the most important thing, but if you go take a part-time job at, say, Home Depot for two years, you will qualify for roughly a $10,000 benefit. And if you do pass on, that same benefit goes straight to your wife." It was just a little extra cushion and some more security for his spouse, who had limited ability to generate more income in the event of his death or another financial emergency. For twenty hours a week, he could buy a little bit of peace for the both of them.

Both of these stories demonstrate why people so rarely approach Social Security with the same level of forethought and preparation they bring to taxes: they simply don't understand how many moving parts the process actually has. Few people even realize that you can actually receive more or less money, depending on what choices you make when you file. Instead, people often assume that filing is a pretty straightforward process with few variables that works just about the same for everyone who does it. You might decide to file at an older or younger age, but beyond that, people assume that everyone does basically the same thing and gets basically the same benefits, controlling for different income histories.

In reality, each filing is potentially as unique as a fingerprint, and taking a one-size-fits-all approach usually means missing out on something or, at best, not knowing if you made a good decision or not. Unfortunately, this is another one of those cases where people often don't know what they're missing because they were never aware of all the possible outcomes of filing. To return to that little mouse in the maze, let's imagine he made some choices, did the best he could, and wound up reaching the end of the maze. For the mouse, that might have felt like a success because he made it out, right? What he didn't know, however, was that there was a big chunk of cheese waiting for him at another exit, which he could have reached via a different route. I can't count the number of times I've had clients come in who didn't even realize they were giving up hundreds, even thousands, of dollars per month because of the way they'd filed.

When we onboard a new client at Watermark Wealth Strategies, we always run an optimization report for them, no matter where they are in the Social Security process. We use a specific software package called "Maximize My Social Security," developed by Dr. Laurence Kotlikoff, an economics professor at Boston University. We selected his program after reviewing the half dozen or so other packages on the market and finding that Dr. Kotlikoff's was by far the most thorough and exact. Kotlikoff himself is something of a Social Security guru, having written three essential books on the subject. The report we generate using Maximize My Social Security gives us an important benchmark, showing us the actual ceiling on what the individual client can receive. And once the mouse knows that cheese is on the table, we can start developing an actual strategy to get out of the maze.

The strategizing process is where having a resource for advice and guidance really becomes invaluable. Just as using the cookie-cutter timeline and filing approach won't necessarily give you the best outcome; neither will purely chasing the highest possible dollar amount. Like everything else about retirement, filing for Social Security has to be a holistic decision that takes into account not only the cold, hard numbers but the human reality of our lives and how we want to live them.

Possibly the best example of this is filing age. Most people are aware that waiting to file until after age seventy results in a bigger Social Security check, but that still doesn't mean that's always the right decision. For some people, waiting nearly a decade may mean having less money during their most active and expensive early retirement years. As I mentioned before when we talked about budgeting, as people get older, their expenses dwindle, and most eighty-four-year-olds aren't sitting in their house thinking, "Thank God I have this extra $400 per month; now I can finally afford to go parasailing in the Caymans!" Just like with our larger budgets, we have to think about Social Security in terms of how we realistically spend money. It's about getting the biggest value, not necessarily the biggest check.

Spending patterns and projections are only one part of the puzzle, though. There's also your spouse's filing to consider, your own work history, your other assets, your projected life span, and your goals for your retirement. You also want to be able to see the impact different choices will have on things like taxes and your other income sources. Having the maximum projection is a bit like getting an entire map of the maze. Not only can we see where the biggest chunk of cheese is, but maybe we can see that there's a little electrified pad we'd have to cross to get to it. With that information, we can make a choice to brave the zaps or maybe go for a different exit. Without the map, we have no way of grading our decisions—or even of making a meaningful decision at all. When right and left are equally obscure, any "choice" you make gives you about as much agency as flipping a coin.

Social Security isn't just important because it provides extra income but because it is one of the few income sources that is guaranteed to come every month until your death. With the decline of pensions across nearly every industry, that kind of retirement security is rare and precious. For someone who is going into retirement with $700,000 to $1 million in investments, Social Security could represent up to 30 or 40 percent of their yearly income. Even for people who have larger yearly incomes, Social Security will probably be the only money they get each month that isn't subject to a rate-of-returns risk, investment risk, or overspending. That check is always going to be there, and when you are gone, it will be there for your spouse too.

We get so few sure things in life (and definitely when it comes to finances) that it's worth taking the time to fully understand and capitalize upon those opportunities that do come our way.

CHAPTER SIX

NET WORTH VERSUS INCOME

Net worth and income are the yin and yang of our financial lives; they are fundamentally different but interrelated, and you need both of them in the correct ratio to have a complete whole. Or, if you prefer car metaphors, net worth and income are like horsepower and torque. Net worth would be your horsepower—it's big and exciting, and more of it is always better. Income, on the other hand, is your torque, which is less flashy but provides consistent power to your wheels. Without horsepower, you'll only be able to crawl along, but without torque, you wouldn't even make it out of your driveway. To get the best ride possible, you want both elements to be working at peak performance.

In more literal terms, net worth is the summary of all your financial "pluses" (houses, cars, investments, other banking products, and account balances) minus all your debts. Income is the amount of money you are adding to that plus column on a regular basis. At different times in our lives, it is most useful to concentrate on one or the other of these, but it's important to always maintain some balance between the two. That balance becomes especially vital when we get to retirement age and the equation changes in a fundamental way.

When you are just starting out in your career, it's both logical and practical to focus mostly on building your income-generating capacity. You also want to grow your overall net worth during this time, but a lot of that growth will happen naturally as a by-product of increasing your income (provided you aren't also scaling your expenses up too steeply). As you get older and advance in your career, most people reach a point where their income plateaus or at least slows in growth, and they turn more of their attention to net worth. This is when a lot of people start looking more seriously into investments and structures to protect their wealth, often with an eye toward retirement. Retirement itself is the fulcrum point where people stop or significantly slow their income from work and instead start living off their accumulated assets.

This basic concept isn't anything new; it's what people are talking about when they say they want to build—or protect—their nest egg, and it's basically the foundational mechanism by which retirement works at all. What does present a problem for people is getting the most from this process. It's not difficult to find a workable balance between income and net worth, especially when you are still in the accumulation phase and you've got money coming in regularly. But it's also not hard to find a workable balance between your horsepower and torque, if you define "workable" as "something that will get you from point A to point B." By that standard, a Yugo is a perfectly workable car, but you would never compare it to, say, a Ferrari. Most of us, if we were picking our ideal driving experience, would probably want something closer to the Ferrari, and the same is true of our financial "engine" as well. Yet when it comes to preparing ourselves for retirement, many people have an income/net worth setup that is a bit more "Eastern European compact" than "sleek Italian racer."

There are basically only two kinds of mistakes you can make with regard to this balancing act, and those are the same mistakes you can make with any balancing act: you can tilt too far in one direction or the other. Yes, there are innumerable ways and reasons you could lean too far, and the consequences will be different, depending on which direction you go. Either way, however, you end up not maximizing your retirement.

If you've ever heard the phrase "house poor," then you've probably heard about the most common way people err on the side of only building net worth. Basically, you know you've invested too much of your assets into growing net worth at the expense of income when it begins to inhibit your cash flow, and it's shockingly easy to do that , especially when it comes to real estate. People want to own homes, especially in America, where people see them as investment vehicles as well as deeply personal possessions. This can make the decision-making around them a bit cloudy, as it gets all bound up with our ideas about families and markers of success, as well as that pesky common wisdom about what everyone "should" do to protect themselves in retirement. Often, people talk themselves into investing more into a home or paying down a mortgage faster than necessary because they have coupled an emotional impulse with a logical, financial justification. Problems arise, however, when people don't see all the implications of transforming liquid cash into a fixed asset with a lot of legal and financial complexities.

There's a thought experiment I like to do with clients to explain how this can become a problem: imagine that you had no money at all, no job, no wealth, a completely clear slate. Then imagine that I, your mysterious benefactor, gave you a $10 million house (I am an extremely generous benefactor in this thought experiment). The house is paid in full; this is a 100 percent free, no-strings-attached house. So you're now $10 million richer, right?

Except you still don't have a job. Your savings account still shows a $0.00 balance, and now you have property taxes, insurance, and upkeep on a $10 million property to pay, to say nothing of heating, electricity, and other utilities. Heck, you don't even have enough money to buy furniture or groceries to fill those empty spaces. Without cash flow to manage regular expenses, a large asset is like a model home: it looks great, and it certainly has intrinsic value, but it's lacking all the things you need to make daily life comfortable or even possible.

After the hard lessons of the 2008 financial crash, it's a bit less common for people to become quite so overleveraged in terms of home buying, but I still see people who take the opportunity to increase the size or caliber of their home, even when it may be the less strategically sound decision. For many of my clients, this comes in the form of aggressively paying down a mortgage. When people approach retirement, they often feel a need to "tie up loose ends," or they begin to feel nagging concerns about debts, even long-term ones like a mortgage. This can drive them to allocate any additional income toward paying down or paying off their home because it feels like the "safest" thing to do.

In reality, focusing on paying down a mortgage can have less impact on your life than you'd imagine and, in the worst-case scenario, can actually make it harder for you to maintain your lifestyle. I've had many clients tell me that they wanted to put their bonus or an inheritance or even just leftover cash at the end of the month toward their mortgage, and I've had to explain to them how their impulse to do the most "responsible" thing may actually be bad for their overall financial health. The client who puts a $50,000 bonus toward his

$300,000 mortgage with ten years left on it believes he's doing the most sensible thing with his excess money, but he hasn't changed his financial situation very much at all. That $50,000 will increase his overall net worth, and each of his subsequent mortgage payments will pay a larger percentage of the principal balance—and those are both great things—but neither really help him at that moment.

That client's mortgage payment, in most cases, will be the same next month, no matter how much he overpays this month (unless, of course, he buys the house outright), and all his other financial obligations will remain the same. Most importantly, investing more money in his house is not increasing his ability to generate income. If his mortgage rate is low, it may be a much better result to invest those funds and generate a return bigger than the mortgage rate. The concept is similar to, say, borrowing money at a rate of 4 percent and investing those funds and earning a return of 6 percent. Clearly earning 6 percent on an investment is better than paying down a mortgage costing you 4 percent.

While real estate can "pay off" in the sense that you may be able to sell a house for more than you paid, paying the house off faster doesn't do anything to increase that future sale price. You could argue that paying down a debt reduces the amount you pay in interest over the life of the debt, but you have to weigh the smaller monthly cost of that interest over the possible complications of "losing" a large chunk of cash at one time.

It is also reasonable to consider how much—and what kind of— value you want and need to get from your home. If you spend a large amount of wealth rapidly paying for a house, it's best to either be confident that you will recoup your money in a future sale or be comfortable with spending the rest of your life in that home. The vagaries of the real estate market make it a pretty volatile way to "invest" your money, and you are often much better off allocating resources to other investment vehicles and simply regarding your house as a place to live.

Not only can people overallocate resources to boosting their net worth, but they can also spend too much on the "wrong kind" of net worth. The perceived "safety" of building net worth can also encourage people to spend more freely on things like vacation properties, second homes, or other large-scale purchases. Then there are high-end consumer goods like expensive cars, boats, or even planes that do technically maintain your net worth on the date of purchase, but often won't appreciate in value themselves. In fact, most of these purchases are assets that depreciate in value each year. These kinds of purchases often happen around retirement because people have been thinking and dreaming about these things for a long time, and retirement was the "finish line" for which they aimed.

People might spend years thinking that if they can just get to retirement, they can finally get that Big Expensive Thing they've always wanted, and it's hard not to prioritize those dreams over the general health of their portfolio. The thing is, in many cases, these purchases aren't inherently impossible or poorly advised; they just need to be made with a full accounting of all the financial implications and with an eye toward timing your retirement income. Diving in headfirst to an array of expensive new projects or hobbies the moment you retire can lead to a painful pinch in your cash flow; as we've discussed before, cash flow for a retiree can't recover from a poorly timed depletion like employment income can.

Oftentimes, having an overbalanced net worth comes from too much caution—people who want to save for a rainy day but don't always recognize that they still have to buy things on the sunny days as well. The other problem—focusing too much on income generation at the expense of net worth—often comes from the opposite impulse. The clients I see who have issues with their income are often the same clients who hadn't done much planning and thinking about retirement. Often, these are people with high incomes, so they didn't have to do the same kind of

> **The simplest and most common mistake people make with income is spending too much of it and not saving enough.**

budgeting in their accumulation phase. Or, at least, they didn't have to budget to stay in the black, even if only barely.

The simplest and most common mistake people make with income is spending too much of it and not saving enough. It's not a complex issue. It sounds so simple because it is, but sometimes the simplest things are the hardest to implement. Different experts will give you different numbers, but in my experience, people should be saving about 20 percent of their gross income on average. That's *gross* … not net.

Now, there are always going to be times in our lives when we are spending more of our income, especially when we are starting out. The saying "you have to spend money to make money" has some truth to it, whether it be moving to a city with better career opportunities, buying a car or wardrobe, or investing in training and education in your field. Additionally, our incomes start small, and regular expenses naturally take up a larger share of them in the beginning. Over time, however, most people should reach a point where they have more flexibility in their budget and need to make decisions about how to allocate their money. If you start investing 20 percent between twenty and thirty years before you plan to retire, you should have a lot of options available by the time that last working day comes. If you really want to become a prodigious accumulator of wealth, up that number to 30 percent!

Some people, however, don't really make those decisions, and it's the absence of a decision more than any conscious choice that leads to a long-term lack of savings. Almost no one I've met consciously wanted to avoid saving money. Most of the time it happens for two reasons: either the person doesn't have enough income to cover their expenses and save, or they never explicitly attempted to earmark money for savings. *You must pay yourself first.* Those who don't have enough income to save typically have a host of other issues when it comes to retirement, so most of my clients fall into the latter category.

> **You must pay yourself first.**

Often, this is a particular problem for people who, on paper, should be doing very well. People with large, comfortable incomes get used to being able to purchase the things they need and want without seeing a negative bank balance, so they don't always have that incentive to dig in and see if they are actually making their money work for them as well as they could be. In the more extreme cases, people even try to "solve" a cash-flow issue not by changing their spending but by increasing their income. Usually, that would be helpful, but not if your spending also increases commensurately, which often happens. To put it another way, if I once again played the generous benefactor and gave this type of person $10 million in cash with no strings attached, they might very well spend it in a few months simply because they were used to withdrawing cash from a constantly replenishing pool. They would end up just as flat broke as the house-poor people but without even the benefits of having a roof over their heads.

Unfortunately, it doesn't have to be wild or irresponsible spending either. I have a client in her early sixties who makes a good living as a medical professional but only has a few hundred thousand saved for retirement. She wasn't buying fur coats and crates of Cristal; she simply didn't track her money very carefully in general, and on top of that, she sent two children to expensive colleges in short succession. That pretty much depleted the small amount she had been able to save—money that had never been specifically earmarked for retirement in the first place. Because she had a well-paying job, lived within her means, and didn't think of herself as a particularly wild spendthrift, she was surprised to find that she had actually fallen well short of her retirement needs.

Not only had my client failed to analyze her finances, but she wasn't analyzing a lot of her spending decisions either. She didn't spend frivolously, and she wasn't in debt, so it hadn't really occurred to her that she even needed a savings strategy or that she should plan her big expenses with the long-term future in mind. Her children's college, for example, probably could have been done in a way that didn't use up so much of her liquid assets. Education is important, and my client wasn't sorry she'd been able to give that to her children, but if I had been advising her at the time, I might have been able to suggest a change in the timing or the structure of her financial contribution that would have allowed her to protect some of her retirement money.

Neither of us have a time machine, however, so we had to work with the situation in front of us. In her case, she had the two basic options that anyone without retirement savings has: she could increase her allocation to savings (either by saving a bigger percentage of her paycheck or by trying to boost that paycheck itself), or she could push off her retirement further into the future. Eventually, we developed a plan that combined both ideas, extending her retirement date while also giving her a more aggressive savings goal to hit. She had all the raw materials she needed to fix her problem; she just wasn't used to saving money as a regular, conscious practice. Once she integrated that into her life, she found that she was still able to live in a normal, comfortable fashion while still making progress on her goals.

Without income, you can't sustain anything; and without net worth, you can't build anything. It's very easy to see some of the big imbalances between the two that I've mentioned in this chapter, but most people have some degree of "tilt" that they might not have noticed. Many people approaching retirement have portfolios that are configured for younger people who can better handle market volatility; others have played it too safe and have a large chunk of their wealth just sitting around in cash and not really earning much for them. Figuring out how exactly to allocate everything is complicated and can be frightening, and people are rightly worried about making a mistake that they can't fix. This can lead them to taking a path of least resistance when it comes to actually structuring their assets to provide retirement income. People will simply withdraw everything they need from the simplest, most accessible source of cash, whether it be a money market account, a savings account, or even a 401(k). If you don't have the underlying structure in place to turn your wealth into an ongoing income stream, however, that money will eventually be depleted.

From a psychological perspective, all of these "mistakes" that people make with their portfolios are completely understandable. It's very common to avoid digging into your finances because it's complex and often frustrating. It's similarly common to feel uncertain and want more security, especially as you approach retirement. The best way to assuage these feelings and to set yourself up for success is to have a clear strategy for your money. A strategy is not the same as a budget, and it's not about setting out specific spending limits and goals for every aspect of your lifestyle (unless, of course, that is what works for you).

Instead, we prefer to work with clients to create guidelines that help them make decisions that bring them closer to their ultimate goals.

That is why we like the 20 percent rule. Generally, if you can set aside 20 percent of your pretax income for investing, you will be setting yourself up for success. When we are trying to get a client properly balanced, we will start by finding that savings goal and working forward from there. We call it "paying yourself," and our rule is that you should always pay yourself first. So if you are making $250,000 per year, you might want to earmark about $50,000 per year for investing. That investment can take whatever form you prefer: investment accounts, retirement accounts, even just a basic savings account if that's what makes you comfortable. After you pay yourself, you pay your bills, and that's where we include all of our nonnegotiable expenses like mortgages, tax payments, any other regular fees and expenses that you require. With both of those things managed, the remainder of the money is entirely at your disposal. I like to say that I don't care if my clients buy five Rolexes a month, provided they've paid themselves the proper amount and paid their bills first.

The 20 percent idea is really just a baseline, however. Each person requires a unique plan of action that accounts for their needs, wants, and means, to say nothing of their individual timeline. Though this kind of strategizing can seem like it's imposing rules on someone, it's actually a very collaborative and even empowering process for most people. There is an extraordinary amount of freedom in knowing you are on track, especially when it is a track you've built yourself. Once you have your savings and expenses locked down, you can and should feel free to spend the rest of that income however you choose.

People who live at the very edge of their means are often simultaneously wracked with uncertainty and guilt about the choices they are making with their money, and much of that comes from a sense of not knowing exactly what kind of impact those choices are having on them. Similarly, people often overinvest because they don't have a good grasp on how much they will need and are afraid of running out of income in the future. A clear, simple guideline not only gives you the assurance of knowing you are on your way to a comfortable retirement but also allows you to check in periodically to make sure that you are still headed in the right direction. Peace of mind can go a long way in the retirement journey.

CHAPTER SEVEN

PENSIONS

If I were writing this book ten or fifteen years in the future, I probably wouldn't even include this chapter. Pensions are kind of like the cassette tapes of retirement-funding vehicles: yes, they definitely still exist, and some older folks really cherish them, but they aren't in common use and most of the under-thirty crowd would have no idea how traditional pensions work. The problem for the next generation of retirees, meaning you, is that pensions weren't exactly replaced by a new product that did the same thing, only more efficiently. The new systems are definitely more complex and often have a much smaller upside for the retiree. So perhaps pensions are more like vinyl: they offered a unique, desirable experience, and many retirees are now trying to use today's tools to recreate yesterday's sound.

Here is a story about pensions that explains why they were so great for an individual and also probably why they were phased out: my father, Bob Liberante, was a schoolteacher in Arizona for about thirty-two years, retiring at the age of fifty-five. That tenure afforded him a pension from the state, which he has now been receiving for thirty-one years. Next year, he will officially have been collecting a pension for as long as he taught. Not only that, but when he does eventually pass away, the pension will go to my mother for the rest of her life. For the Liberantes, this is a great deal—not so much for the State of Arizona.

The problem inherent in pensions is one of the overarching problems of retirement that we talked about before: all of these systems were designed for a population with a much shorter life span. My father is a bit of an outlier, as he both retired earlier than average and is exceeding the average life span (though not by much; the life expectancy of a middle-class white man in America is in the low eighties), but his situation is not uncommon. Especially when you factor in pensions that transfer to a spouse, you can see how companies and other entities would balk at paying former employees twenty, thirty, or even forty years beyond their last working day.

The earliest pension plans were part of the benefits afforded to retired soldiers, combined with the widespread "widows' pensions," which were exactly what they sounded like. Eventually, government and civil-service jobs began incorporating pensions, and some private corporations followed. In America, the real pension heyday didn't kick off until WWII. A lot of different factors contributed to their rise: pensions were a good way to attract and retain employees when wartime privations made it hard to increase wages; labor unions were also proliferating at the time, and pensions were a desirable benefit; and pensions fit nicely with the new model of work that would continue into the '50s and '60s—that of the "company man" who worked his way up in one organization from which he would eventually retire. By 1960, roughly 50 percent of private sector employees had a pension.

The '80s represented a nadir of pensions, especially in the private sector, and it's likely no accident that this roughly coincided with the first waves of retirees beginning to draw their benefits. One of the biggest problems with pensions, both for those drawing them and those delivering them, is the issue of future uncertainty. Pensions are popular and common in public service and military positions because those are entities that can be reasonably certain they will continue to exist in more or less the same form indefinitely. The State of Arizona may not love the fact that is has to send my dad a check every month, but there's no reasonable worry that it is going to cease to be a state, or run out of funds and thus be unable to send that check. At least, that's what I might have said a few years ago. As it turns out, there are some states that, due to poor financial planning and budgeting, are struggling to deal with their looming pension obligations. If even a large, stable bureaucracy like a state government can run into these problems, imagine how fraught private pension plans can become.

In the 1970s, a number of regulations were passed to protect pensions in the event that a corporation's pension fund failed, but there's only so much that can be done by law. If you spend forty years working for XYZ Corp and its pension goes bankrupt the day after you retire, there just isn't much recourse for the average person—the government can't simply conjure up money that no longer exists. You would then be forced into the Pension Benefit Guaranty Corporation, which would only provide you with a fraction of your original pension benefit. When this happened—and it did happen with a devastating regularity—it was big news, to the point where many people began to lose confidence in the security of their own pension plans.

On the other side, many companies began to see pensions as a mounting obligation that they might not be able to meet in an unknown future. Pensions are basically a debt owed by a company for an indefinite amount of time to be repaid under unknown conditions, and that is a huge amount of risk. Companies naturally began to restructure their retirement benefits in an attempt to shift some of that risk back on to the employees.

As all this was happening, we were also seeing a change in how Americans—both at the individual and corporate level—thought about work and careers, especially white-collar careers. Companies were less concerned with "developing" a lifelong employee, and it began to be more common for people to move around regularly within an industry—or even between industries. This mutual decrease in career loyalty arguably began to happen as early as the late '60s, and the modern gig economy is perhaps the culmination of this model of work. It was actually a lot of blue-collar industries like agriculture or manufacturing that did the most to encourage lifelong employment and set the standard for the traditional model of a "good job" that one could occupy from college (often even from high school) to retirement. But many of these industries, while still significant parts of the economy, are no longer major employers. For example, more than 30 percent of all employed people in 1960 worked in the manufacturing sector; today it is less than 10 percent. Those jobs have largely been replaced by jobs in the service sector, which can range from education to retail, and a lot of these industries have not traditionally offered pensions.

Instead, what we began to see were things like 401(k) plans and other defined contribution plans. "Defined contribution" is in contrast to "defined benefit" plans, which are the types of plans most people imagine when they hear the word "pension." *Defined benefit* simply means that the employer and employee enter into the pension agreement with the understanding that the employer will pay a defined amount of money (usually either a fixed sum or a percentage of their yearly salary) as a monthly stipend for the employee in retirement. Defined contribution plans turn that idea around—the employee pays an amount of their choosing into an account—often a 401(k)—and typically, the employer matches that amount, within certain limits. But the end result is no longer known or guaranteed.

The selling point of this type of plan for an employee is the increased control one has over their retirement fund. With a traditional or defined benefit pension, the employee doesn't see or interact with the money until they retire and start getting checks. With a 401(k) or other defined contribution plan, an employee can allocate their money to different products offered by the funds and manage their investment, as well as controlling how much they want to contribute. Often, 401(k)s are more flexible than traditional pensions and can be liquidated prior to retirement. For all these reasons, 401(k)s are often pitched as a way to more independently secure a large stream of income for retirement.

The biggest downside to these plans is, of course, the primary reason they've become so widespread in the first place: they put a significant amount of risk on the employee's plate. You have to be responsible for managing and correctly allocating your assets; you have to pay into the account to get the matching bonus, and you are exposed to the risk that comes with any sort of market investment.

While the more open-ended nature of these plans also makes it possible to get a bigger overall yield than with a traditional pension, you give up the safety net a pension provides. If you invest poorly or happen to run into a sequence-of-returns snag, there's nothing in a 401(k) to protect your money or to help you recoup a loss. With an old-school pension, you don't have to worry about how the stock market is doing and whether you retired in a growing economy or one that is receding. You could have the worst luck in the world and retire just as the stock market peaks and is starting to fall, and the same check will still show up in your mailbox every month.

Let's walk through a scenario. Imagine that there are twin sisters preparing to retire. One worked as a public servant for thirty years and is eligible to draw a pension that is a percentage of her salary. The other started her own business and then sold it with a $2 million lump sum she put into savings. If you averaged out their working lives, they made roughly the same amount of money; the only major difference is the form in which they take it into retirement. Now, which do you imagine is having the more comfortable retirement experience? On one hand, the public servant is getting about $10,000 per month, which covers most of her expenses comfortably. The other sister needs to get a 6 percent average yearly return from her $2 million to make that same monthly income. To get that 6 percent, the business-owner sister has to manage and calibrate her portfolio; she has to deal with the constant questions about whether she's doing everything correctly, whether it will be enough, how she can compensate if she has a bad month or two, and so forth. It's not just about the money you have, but about knowing how to safely turn that pile of money into a reliable income stream.

On the other hand, if the public-servant sister wanted to buy a new car six months after she retired, she would have to save a portion of her pension check each month until she had enough. The business-owner sister would have the freedom to simply take the money out of her savings account and buy the car right away. If you are someone who values that flexibility, the pension may not meet all of your needs. Fortunately, there are actually several products available that can provide a pension-like income stream with a little more flexibility (some of which I'll address in the next chapter).

It's important to remember that, like almost every other element of retirement savings, there are customizable options, and you don't have to go with the most common, most traditional, or most anything if it isn't beneficial for you. The 401(k) is a great example of this. Despite its current ubiquity, it's actually a pretty new retirement product and is not very well understood by a lot of the people who have it. It was designed to be a supplement to other types of retirement income, especially for people in high-level corporate positions who wanted a way to save more each year on a pretax basis. In the thirty or so years it has existed, it has been applied widely and relied upon as if it were a tried-and-tested solution. It has been treated like a replacement for the pension, when it is really only one part of a much larger puzzle that only gets more intricate each year.

I've talked often in this book about how people can fall into "passive" forms of retirement preparation. A major reason why that happens is that, for a long time, a successful retirement simply required less effort and management on the part of the individual. For decades, a person could work steadily at a job and pay their taxes and be assured that, when they retired at the appropriate time, they would receive a pension and Social Security stipend that provided for most, if not all, of their needs. Usually those benefits would roll over to their spouse upon the person's death as well, so they didn't even have to spend a lot of time thinking about legacy planning. People could always save more, but those two funding sources were the basic bedrock of retirement, and the average employee didn't have to do anything more complicated than signing the occasional form to make it happen. Now, there is a lot of onus on the individual to essentially DIY their own pension using careful investing, strategic savings, and often the advice of a good financial planner. Arguably, my industry would not have grown as much as it has in the past thirty years or so had pensions not gone the way of the dodo bird.

ANNUITIES

This may very well be the most controversial chapter in the book, and while what I'm about to say may seem extreme, I urge you to hear me out before you throw this book away in disgust. With that said, here it is, my most shocking financial opinion:

Annuities are useful tools that more people should consider including in their retirement planning.

Unfortunately, annuities have gotten a very bad rap over the past few years, to the point where even mentioning them is enough to shut down a conversation with some clients. Not only has the product itself come to be seen as practically radioactive, but financial advisors who suggest them are also regarded with suspicion. People react to the idea of investing in an annuity the same way they might react to a used car salesman giving them the hard sell.

To explain exactly how this state of affairs came about, I have to tell you what annuities are designed to do and how they have been used—and misused—in the financial industry. That reticence people have about annuities isn't entirely misplaced, but once again, like most common wisdom and rules of thumb, it also overlooks a lot of nuance.

The situation is similar to the US car industry in the early '80s when the Chrysler corporation was turning out some of the poorest-quality cars on the market. They seemed to come right off the factory line with problems built in. Did this mean we should stop driving cars? Should we go back to the horse-drawn carriage? Or was a better approach to stop driving Chryslers? There were plenty of other carmakers making very high-quality cars and trucks. America still needed transportation; the solution was to buy a car manufactured by a better carmaker. This same is true of annuities, and just like Chrysler, many annuity companies have drastically improved the quality of the ride.

The problem, if you want to call it that, is that annuities come in all shapes and sizes, and while one may be a perfect fit for a client, another may look totally different and have almost no positive impact on a client's retirement plan. Yet both products wear the annuity badge, so it is easy to see how a person could be confused about the value of such a product.

An annuity is a financial product designed primarily for retirement (though it has other uses). It is mainly intended to solve some of the problems we've discussed before concerning a lack of regular infusions of income after work ends. There are many types of annuities, and broadly speaking, any product that offers a series of regular payments counts as an annuity. Social Security is an annuity, as are traditional pensions. Most of the annuities I work with as a financial planner, however, are issued by life insurance companies.

I am not an across-the-board advocate for annuities (or any product, honestly), and I freely admit there are a lot of badly designed annuities out there. It isn't difficult to get a license that allows you to sell annuities. You don't even have to be a financial professional to do it—in theory, you could be a plumber by day, annuity salesperson by night if that's what you wanted to do. Along with a glut of people who are legally capable of selling them (though perhaps not of fully understanding them or giving any broader financial advice), annuities have become notorious for offering huge commissions for these salespeople. This creates two big problems: 1) less-scrupulous financial professionals are pushing these products not because they are a good fit for the client but because they want a big commission, and 2) a range of additional fees is passed to the client to generate said big commission. Some of the most exploitative annuities have extremely long surrender schedules— sometimes twenty years or more—and, of course, the financial penalty for withdrawing money early is also extremely high. This combines to create a rock-and-a-hard-place situation for the client, who is either getting gouged by poor performance, regular maintenance fees, or early withdrawal penalties.

The proliferation of this type of product, which is really more a cash grab for an institution and salespeople, is a big part of what has made "annuity" such a dirty word in the world of retirement planning. Consumers

> Annuities are an excellent retirement product for lots of people—when they are used properly and the proper product is selected.

are right to be somewhat skeptical and to protect themselves, but avoiding annuities altogether isn't the best answer for many retirees. It would be a bit like deciding that because some used car salespeople misrepresent the conditions of their cars and the nature of their contracts, all used cars are bad and anyone selling them is a scammer. A great many used cars are in excellent condition and are a completely viable solution for someone who needs an affordable vehicle. Similarly, annuities are an excellent retirement product for lots of people—when they are used properly and the proper product is selected.

The fundamental problems with annuities are not unique to those products. If I were to explain to you how stocks, bonds, or mutual funds worked using only the examples of brokerages, fund managers, and institutions exploiting their clients, you would probably have a similarly dark view of those products. Unfortunately, there's an element of risk with any method of saving or investing money, and there's almost always a way for some enterprising person to capitalize on that risk for their own personal gain. There's no such thing as a completely safe—or entirely dangerous—financial product. They are all just tools, and instead of simply ignoring some of them, it is far more useful to carefully evaluate each tool and become educated on the options so you can make a well-informed decision.

There are definitely people out there who think primarily of what will benefit them instead of what will benefit the client and act accordingly. I would argue, however, that the bigger danger is people who aren't necessarily looking to "scam" anyone but simply lack knowledge and haven't realized what they are missing. In the case of annuities, for example, many of the people who warn to never, ever use an annuity are not even licensed to sell them and often don't know much more about them than a moderately well-read layperson.

One of the big problems with exploitative annuities is financial advisors who only have an insurance license required to sell annuities but don't have other forms of licensure to offer different products. Because they only had one tool in their box, that was what they pushed for in every situation—it was the old problem of everything looking like a nail when all you have is a hammer. But that doesn't make the reverse any better. If an advisor cannot sell annuities, they are disincentivized to suggest them for clients in the same way someone who can only sell annuities is incentivized. Plus, if they haven't bothered to go through the licensing procedure, it's fair to question how fully they understand the product. Sometimes, the problem really is a nail, and you can't insist it's a screw instead just because you never bothered to buy a hammer. The solution, which we have embraced at Watermark Wealth Strategies, is to stock our toolbox with every tool we can find. This allows us to evaluate every situation based on the problem that needs solving, rather than simply looking at it through the lens of which solutions we are equipped to provide.

The best way to protect yourself in financial matters—as in most matters, honestly—is to educate yourself and gather information. When you are approaching a financial planner, take a close look at how their company is structured, what they can and can't do, and, most importantly, how they make their money. You particularly want to watch out for lopsided financial incentives that make one product way more "profitable" for a person or company. At Watermark, for example, we try to make product choices revenue neutral for our firm. This is not always possible, but if there is a conflict, we make sure our clients know that commission difference and even have them sign a document showing how much we are compensated from the annuity provider. So a client could pay us 1 percent a year to manage their assets, or an annuity company can pay us 1 percent per year to manage the annuity, and there's no incentive for me personally either way. The only reason I would suggest one route over another for a client is if I think it would genuinely be the better option for their situation. At the end of the day, the biggest incentive I have is to protect my clients' assets and their income, and I want to make that clear to them.

One good way of separating the wheat from the chaff is looking for Certified Financial Planners. This is a specific professional certification that financial planners are not required to get, so if someone has it, it suggests they are willing to go that extra step to add tools to their toolbox. CFPs are also governed by a code of professional ethics that requires them to place their clients' interests above their own. And, as heretical it might seem to some people, that sometimes means putting a client in an annuity.

Annuities are a powerful way to address the sequence-of-return problem that plagues so many retirees, and in its most basic form, it is a risk-reduction tool. Many people benefit not just from the actual income stream but from the security of knowing that income stream will be available when they need it. Annuities are often dinged for the limitations they have, but that thinking really overlooks how important stability and predictability is, especially when it comes to retirement income.

It's also important to consider that, like every other financial product, annuities have developed a lot over time. Many people still think of annuities in terms of what their parents or grandparents owned when the modern annuity landscape is completely different. In fact, that's often another point of friction when it comes to broaching the topic of annuities—so many people are working with an outdated understanding of what they are or can do.

The hypothetical example I like to use is that of a cell phone. If someone asked you, "Hey, want a free cell phone?" you would probably say yes. Consider that this person then went on to describe this "cell phone," saying, "Well, the phone comes in this briefcase that you have to carry with you everywhere, and the whole thing weighs eight pounds. Also, the reception's not great, and every call costs $2.50 a minute. Do you still want one?" That would be an entirely different situation, wouldn't it? Of course you wouldn't want that nearly useless briefcase phone; you were expecting a smartphone, a powerful computer that fits in your pocket and costs pennies to talk on—you know, a cell phone.

Except that the briefcase phone is just as much of a "cell phone" as the iPhone X is; it just dates from an earlier stage of technological development. Cell phones are so ubiquitous that, aside from the occasional rogue time traveler, we mostly know what someone means when they talk about a cell phone (or even a phone at this point). With something like annuities, however, knowledge is much more specialized, and many people's conception of them is trapped in the briefcase-cell era.

So for those clients who may have outdated or overly narrow understandings of what annuities are, I like to get rid of that word entirely. Instead, I want to tell them about a new and exciting financial product, which has a number of features that could benefit them. Let's call it … a b-nnuity.

Imagine you are preparing to retire and you decide to take $300,000 of your million-dollar 401(k), and you're going to put it into a b-nnuity. It's going to pay you, let's say, 5 percent of that investment every year for the rest of your life. It will never pay you less than that for as long as you are alive, regardless of whether the actual investment grows or decreases in value. That already sounds pretty good, right? Wait until you hear the next part: if your investment does happen to grow, however, you get a raise, and once you get that raise, it becomes a permanent part of your guaranteed lifetime income. So now you're maybe getting 5.2 percent of your $300,000, and you are getting that until your death. And if the market goes up again next year? You might get another raise, and you might wind up seeing 5.5 percent or more for the rest of your life. This b-nnuity is like an elevator without any down buttons: once you climb to a floor, you can only go farther up. You are no longer in any danger of falling.

I'm using somewhat arbitrary, though certainly not extraordinary, numbers in this example, but I've seen real-life situations where people reaped an even greater advantage than the hypothetical person in my example. I have a client who recently locked in a 27 percent gain overall in their Unnamed Financial Product, and the market happened to hit a high three days before the anniversary of their initial purchase, which is when the yearly "credit" is calculated. This gave them approximately $80,000 more than they were expecting. There was a little bit of luck involved, as there always is when it comes to the market, but it was the years of patiently "leveling up" that allowed them to really make the most of that happy accident. Another client of mine is only in their third year owning an Unnamed Financial Product, and their income is already up to 14 percent from where they started.

Even if the market tanks tomorrow, those clients will still be guaranteed that income at the increased level. Even if their actual account runs out of money, they still get a disbursement at the same rate every month until they both die, just like a pension. However, if they don't zero out their account before they pass, their b-nnuity is structured so that the remaining value will be passed along to their heirs, just like any other assets.

This is the kind of product I'm talking about when I say that more people should consider integrating annuities into their retirement planning. It isn't larded up with fees and big up-front commissions; the surrender schedule and provisions regarding how the fund is distributed are sensible and beneficial to the client, and it offers real peace of mind for people who are trying to build an entirely new income from their existing assets. Best of all, it offers a real chance at some reasonable income growth within that secure framework. One of the more legitimate criticisms of annuities is that they are not really "money-making" products, meaning they don't get the kind of returns someone can get from other savings or investments vehicles. My counter to this is twofold. The first part is, as I've mentioned, the fact that most annuities are not really products for a thirty-year accumulation phase. They exist primarily to protect and parcel out your income to ensure you have a regular stipend during retirement, not to build up your capital. The second argument is that, though some annuities do have a reduced potential for growth, the extensive protection features baked into a good annuity can make for a long-term gain that is equal or even greater than a product with bigger returns and bigger vulnerabilities.

Perhaps one of the greatest protective features of the annuity is, I think, actually an unintended by-product of its structure. When people have that income guarantee, it insulates them from some of the panic that can cause folks to prematurely pull money out of an investment. An annuity is designed so people can kind of forget about it, and because you can get a piece of the upside with none of the downside, it rewards people for staying the course. Countless studies have shown that it is that very ability—the willingness to maintain an investment for a prolonged period of time—that allows for greater returns over time.

The average mutual fund has an 8 to 10 percent rate of return over time (admittedly better than most annuities, certainly at the time of purchase). However, the average investor in those funds only actually receives between 2 and 3 percent. At first glance, that just seems mathematically impossible. How can people be getting such a small slice of the pie? It's because people enter and exit those investments at the wrong time. They get in when it's high, hoping for even greater success and bail out when it inevitably dips—they aren't staying long enough to complete the full cycle and get all the possible growth. This is a problem caused by fear. People are afraid of missing out on the next big thing, so they buy into something at a peak and they are afraid of losing all their money, so they get out at the first major downturn.

I've talked before about how important it is to manage fear and prevent panic when planning for retirement, and annuities are an excellent way to do that. Accepting the limitations of the product and the more modest growth potential reduces a lot of that financial FOMO, and the income guarantee eliminates the panic that comes from watching your investment dwindle away in an unfavorable market. Annuities, to me, represent one of the most important parts of financial planning: it's not just about the numbers. When we build a retirement plan, we need to account for human behavior and human needs, and the product with the greatest possible theoretical "payoff" isn't always the one that will ease our minds or make our lives easier.

As we were in the final stages of editing this book, our world was hit with the coronavirus pandemic. Consequently, the first quarter of 2020 was the worst-performing quarter the stock market had ever seen in history. Pandemics are not something financial advisors are trained to predict, but as one may imagine or hope, a good financial advisor plans for the unknown because we know financial storms will come. Their cause is not relevant. What is relevant is the real impact those storms have on people's financial lives. A lot of our clients had a good portion of their investments protected in products that did not lose any money or impact their income, even though this was the worst quarter in financial history. I can tell you that when we discussed these products with them, they were very happy they had a portion of their accounts protected. Would you be surprised to learn these products have the moniker of annuity attached to them?

Annuities are one option in a crowded field, and among annuities themselves, there are so many different varieties. Some are excellent, some are perfectly good for one person and not right for another, some are genuinely bad and should be avoided. The prohibition on them reminds me a bit about those popular food science "rules" that seem to cycle around regularly. Remember when fat was the worst thing you could put in your body? As it turns out, dietary fat is pretty important and, in the correct quantities and from the correct sources, extremely beneficial to the human body. Cutting out fat may seem easier than learning about nutrition and applying it to one's specific situation, but in the long run, it means missing out on a lot of good (sometimes even vital) stuff.

The lesson of the annuity is the same lesson we learn from all those "one simple tricks" and "surefire hacks" in life: efforts to simplify a complex situation into easy rules are often going to come up short because some things in life just are that personalized and complicated and really do require thoughtful, educated solutions.

CHAPTER NINE:

GOOD DEBT VERSUS BAD DEBT

If I were making a list of questions that clients regularly ask me over the course of their retirement planning, "Should I pay off my house?" would probably be in the top five. Whenever someone receives an inheritance or other windfall, it inevitably comes up. It's usually one of the first things people want to talk about when we discuss building an asset structure or a timeline for their retirement. Basically, the only people who never ask about it are those who don't have a mortgage!

I find two things particularly interesting about this phenomenon. One is how, no matter how different the circumstances or personalities, something about a mortgage in particular seems to weigh on people's minds. I've known clients who had much more pressing issues still getting hung up on the house questions, and I've seen people for whom their mortgage presents no encumbrance whatsoever still worried about it. My own parents are in the latter camp. They have a small mortgage on their house that has seemingly never hindered them from doing anything they want to do. They payments are extremely manageable, and they have no intention of moving houses or buying other property. Yet I have, more than once, caught my mom making double payments on the house for no reason that I could see. It wasn't a practical decision for my mother; it was emotional. Even though it didn't negatively impact her life in any measurable way, the mortgage bothered her; it was like a pebble in her shoe.

The other thing I find interesting is how everyone who asks me this question seems to think there's one empirically correct solution. As my mother's example indicates, the question of whether or not someone should pay off their mortgage almost always depends on how that person feels about their mortgage. If it were simply a matter of running the numbers, the clients probably wouldn't need to ask me at all. You don't need specialized financial training to see that the money you "lose" on the 3 to 5 percent interest rates we see in most mortgages today is much less than the returns you'd get from putting that money into a good investment vehicle. In general, if you aren't struggling to make the payment and don't have some sort of wildly inflated interest rate, keeping your mortgage and investing the "excess" money is always going to be the mathematically correct option.

I tell you all of this to illustrate how nebulous the concept of "good" and "bad" debt can be for many people. For many of us—my mother, for example—"good debt" is a contradiction in terms. Debt is an inherently bad thing to be avoided or eliminated as soon as possible.

Not all debts are created equal. That's a very common mindset, especially among older generations, and there's a lot of merit in it. It's a protective way of approaching one's finances that helps people keep their lifestyle from ballooning beyond the limits of their income. Of course, it's virtually impossible to completely avoid at least some type of debt over the course of one's financial life, and that's where this kind of thinking can limit people.

Not all debts are created equal. The classic, though somewhat flexible, definition of "good debt" is any debt you incur purchasing something that will appreciate over time. Sometimes, features of the debt itself, like the interest rates and flexibility, can make a debt "better" or "worse." Student loan debt, for example, has historically been considered "good debt" not only because the original purchase (higher education) theoretically offers a significant return on your investment in the future, but also because many educational loans, especially those serviced by the federal government, have quite low interest rates. As we've seen in recent years, however, many student loans haven't delivered the expected upside for borrowers, and the near impossibility of discharging that type of debt can make them burdensome. Even "good" debt is often very situation-dependent, but in general, if you are taking on debt in order to grow a business or make a solid investment, it probably counts as "good."

I opened this chapter talking about mortgages because buying a house is one of the classic ways to incur good debt. For one thing, we all have to live somewhere, so if you're going to pay for housing, it's not a bad idea to own it. Also, even with the fluctuations in the real estate market, the price of houses tends to go up over time, especially when we're talking in terms of the average mortgage lengths (twenty-five, thirty years or more). A mortgage gives you the immediate value of having a roof over your head and the future benefit of being able to sell that house for more than you paid (ideally). It also gives you a certain amount of flexibility because, instead of plunking down a huge chunk of your total assets to buy the house, you can pay a manageable sum each month and use the rest of that money in other ways. Even buying more than one house can be a good investment, especially if you are planning to use it as a rental property.

By contrast, the hallmark of bad debt is something that will not appreciate in value (or will even depreciate). My go-to example of this is automobile debt. While it's true that, as with a house, most people need a vehicle either way, cars notoriously only depreciate in value. They aren't an investment like a house; they are a pure utility (or, in some cases, a luxury). Considering that, many automobile loans cost much more than they offer in value, and they are notorious for having high interest rates. The longer you maintain a car loan, the worse it actually becomes as an investment; you want to either buy a car outright or pay off the loan as quickly as possible if you are carrying a high interest rate.

As I mentioned above, student loan debt kind of straddles the border of good and bad here, depending on the nature of the loans, of the education purchased, and of the borrower themselves. The value that a student loan "buys" you isn't as tangible as a house, and there are even more variables at play than in the real estate market. Most people would say something like law school, for example, is a good reason to incur debt, yet many recent law school grads are struggling to find work, as full-time legal employment is currently at a thirty-year low. These people made what appeared to be a solid financial decision (and, possibly, it may still be that in the long run), and they could not have predicted an unprecedented slump in the employment market. Similarly, the rising cost of tuition at both the graduate and under-graduate level has changed the calculus on this type of "investment" for many people. Still, statistics show that people with a four-year degree earn more than twice what someone without a college degree earns over the course of their working lives, and going on to a master's or PhD offers a 20 percent increase over that.

Possibly the worst type of debt is credit card debt, and not just because it has some of the highest and most unstable interest rates of all these options. Credit card debt is particularly dangerous because it's almost designed to be forgettable. Entities that deal in mortgages, student loans, and automobile loans ultimately want you to pay back those debts—that's how they make their money in the end. Credit card companies thrive on nonrepayment of debt. They love it when you carry a balance, and they get to charge 18 percent to 21 percent interest on it. The system works when people rack up debt unthinkingly and then allow it to linger, accumulating more and more interest. At least, it works for the credit card companies when that happens.

Credit card debt has a way of slipping people's mind the way a mortgage or a car payment doesn't, possibly because it's harder to connect that money owed to one singular thing that it purchased. When your "loan" represents an amalgam of purchases from morning coffee to gym memberships, it's hard to think of it as one investment like a house or a car. I've had people come to our office on multiple occasions proudly telling me that they were going to allocate some extra money to paying off a car loan with 3 percent interest while completely ignoring the $20,000 they had sitting on a credit card with a 19 percent rate.

Credit cards aren't evil, though. They're just a powerful tool—as is debt in general—and, like with most powerful tools, if you use it improperly, you can hurt yourself. When deployed thoughtfully and prudently, debt can enhance your net worth and your life in general. When used carelessly, it can make you a slave. I've seen it happen to so many people: they get caught in a job and don't have the freedom to move or try something new because they are struggling under a huge debt load. Particularly in my line of work, I've known people who can't retire on the timeline they'd prefer because they still have too much debt hanging over their heads.

The majority of my clients aren't quite that restricted by debt. For most of them, it all comes back to that question at the top of the chapter: Should I pay off my house? And to that question, I don't really have an answer. To a certain degree, the quality of your debt is in the eye of the beholder, and I can't tell someone else what their priorities or feelings are about their own personal situation. If you are someone who is looking to increase your net worth, it's probably wiser to leave your mortgage be and concentrate on funding investments with higher rates of return. If you are someone who is thinking of moving to a different state (or country!) in your retirement, maybe don't bother paying down the mortgage, and start preparing to find another property. If you are the sort of person who wakes up at night thinking about your monthly house payment, however, maybe the peace of mind is worth it.

In the end, the question that my clients are asking me is really a question for themselves, and that's how I frame all these conversations. I recently met with a younger couple who were only in their forties but had just gotten a large amount of money after selling their business. They were trying to decide how to allocate this money—specifically whether or not they should pay off their small mortgage. Obviously, as a financial advisor, it would have been in my best interest to have them invest all that money, and arguably, that was what was economically best for them as well. Instead of telling them that, however, I asked them some questions.

"What makes you comfortable? Does having a house payment really bother you guys? Do you worry about it now that you've sold your business and have a lower income? Does your monthly payment bother you guys every month, and do you feel tight on money? Or do you not feel that way, and you really want your money to grow faster?"

We went through all these avenues, but the two of them were still struggling. Eventually, with just a few minutes left in the meeting, I looked at the wife and said, "Gut reaction: pay it off or not?"

"Pay it off," she said immediately, and I turned to the husband, who nodded. I could tell from their faces that, deep down, this was the answer they'd been seeking all along. They didn't want me to tell them what was best for them; they wanted me to help validate their instincts and their needs. They wanted me to give them permission to do what would make them happiest.

At the end of the day, that is the guiding principle of retirement management: How can I help you live the life you want? Forty years from now, I could run the numbers on that couple and their finances, and maybe I could show them that their mortgage payment would have made more had we invested it. But the converse is also true: we could have taken that money and put it into some product that lost 25 percent of its value in three months because of a blip in the market. The potential gain would not have impacted their life all that much, but the loss probably would have kept them up at night. Good debt isn't good when it preys on your mind and adds to your worries. Sometimes you have to pause in your journey and shake that pebble out of your shoe. Maybe it won't make the journey any faster, but it will make it a whole lot more comfortable.

CHAPTER TEN:

INSURANCE

Do you remember how old you were when you first heard about the concept of insurance? Maybe it was on a late-night infomercial or your parents lamenting the rise in their premiums when you started driving. For most people, however, their first real understanding of insurance comes out of some life-changing event. If you're lucky, it's something positive like a marriage or the impending birth of a child that reminds you of all the things that depend upon you and your good health. If you're unlucky, it's an unexpected tragedy that demonstrates just how fleeting and unpredictable life can be.

Young people are notorious for behaving as though they are invincible, and as we age, we are slowly disabused of that notion. We start to rack up injuries; we see near-misses turn into bad outcomes for people we know and love. Slowly, we begin to understand that bad things really do happen to good people and that we have a limited ability to control all the possible outcomes of a situation. Even then, it's still difficult to map that onto ourselves and face the reality of our own vulnerabilities in the world. Sometimes, though, the world has a way of shocking us out of that complacency.

I'm a road-biking enthusiast, and I've been doing it for years now, long enough to build up a network of friends who also love the sport. It's not without its danger because you are sharing the road with cars and accidents do happen, even when you're careful. A few years back, some of my riding friends were out on a ride we have done countless times. On the descent, a car attempted to pass going up a mountain road. He struck one of my fellow cyclists head-on and killed him almost instantly. It was a horrible, traumatic incident, not in the least because it could have been any one of us. The man who died wasn't doing anything wrong; he just happened to be in the wrong place at the wrong time. If he'd been a few yards further ahead, maybe he would have had the time to swerve out of the way.

In the aftermath of that terrible accident, I was talking with one of the other guys who had been on the trip that day, a young guy named Brendon, who had just told us all that his wife was expecting their first child. "Brendon," I asked him, "do you and your wife have life insurance yet?" It was something I'd been meaning to ask but, after what had just happened, it took on a special urgency.

"Not yet. I need to get it," he said, the way people sometimes say they need to make time to watch the latest prestige TV series.

"Yes," I said, "you do. You know, the same thing could happen to any of us, and you've got a child to think about now. We can do it for you at Watermark if you want."

He brightened. "Really? I didn't know you did that sort of thing."

"Sure," I said. As it turned out, he had been thinking about life insurance but just didn't know how to go about getting it; what he needed was an easy access point. We ended up getting a policy for both himself and his wife, nothing too flashy or expensive but enough to ensure that the other person could manage should anything happen to them. I didn't make the offer to him that day as a sales pitch, and if he had told me that he wasn't comfortable getting the policy from my firm, I would have been happy to point him to some other good options. I asked

> People put off dealing with insurance for another day, and then another and another. Sometimes, however, we run out of days.

him out of a genuine desire to help him protect his family because I knew from experience how often people put off dealing with insurance for another day, and then another and another. Sometimes, however, we run out of days.

Not only can it be challenging for people to start the process of getting life insurance, but many people also don't realize that their insurance needs to be modified over the course of their life as their needs change. It all comes down to risk and how it evolves as we age. For someone like Brendon and his wife, the risk is obvious: If I die, how will my spouse replace my income and provide for our child? In twenty or so years, however, their risk will have changed. Often, the level and nature of their insurance coverage will not have kept up with those shifting priorities.

For example, my twenty-five-year-old child will not need the same level of protection and financial support from me as my two-year-old child (at least one would hope …). That is why many young people purchase "term life insurance" which, as the name implies, lasts for a period of time, say twenty years. This means that, if anything happens to you in the first twenty years of your child's life, they are going to have a financial cushion to make sure they can still maintain an acceptable living situation until they reach adulthood and can support themselves.

Once they reach the end of the term (where, presumably, they will be more self-sufficient), that policy simply stops.

Term life insurance basically exists to serve that demand for a temporary version of life insurance that allows people to only cover the time when their dependents are most vulnerable and in need of financial protection. This is in contrast to "whole life insurance," which is what most people think of when they think of life insurance. With a whole life policy, you pay premiums every month, and the policy pays out when you die, no matter how old you or your beneficiaries are at that point. A lot of people (especially people who are retirement aged) carry policies like this—not to cover the gaps that would be left were they to pass away, but as another type of inheritance they can leave to their spouse or children. This is a very basic example of the different ways insurance can be modified for different needs but, even within these types of products, there's a lot of fine-tuning and personalization one can do, if one knows those options are on the table.

Also, while life insurance is perhaps the most well-known type of insurance (not to mention the one most people are likely to prioritize), it's actually just one small piece of the big risk-management puzzle. There's also health insurance, which is an especially large concern for people approaching retirement and worried about incurring medical expenses. Plus, there are things like liability insurance for businesses, rental properties, and other assets and disability insurance for cases of catastrophic injury. Having an insurance plan or structure in place isn't just about buying one kind of policy—it's about making sure you've mitigated as much risk as is both possible and reasonable.

"Reasonable" is very important when it comes to insurance because it's very easy for someone to become lopsided—overinsured in one area and underinsured in another. The average person isn't an expert at risk assessment and may not know all the ways they can be at risk. Often, they simply choose coverage based on the common wisdom, what they've seen peers do, or even just their gut feelings about where they are most vulnerable. The fact that everyone's life situations and associated risks are constantly evolving also means that, if someone doesn't regularly monitor their overall insurance situation, they can wind up with a plan that is more suited to their life as it was five, ten, or twenty years before.

One of the most common ways I see people overinsure is actually via those whole life policies I mentioned before. People buy policies at a much younger age and simply hold on to them without ever really evaluating how useful the potential payout might be at a future point in their lives. Often, the premiums for these policies are taking too much of their monthly income, and even if they paid out tomorrow, their spouse likely wouldn't need the level of financial support the policies provide. Their spouse may not even live long enough themselves to use the vast majority of the money. They might be much better served spending that extra monthly income in the present when both spouses can enjoy it.

For people who are using the policies to provide a kind of additional inheritance, I often suggest doing a more straightforward type of estate planning that doesn't put such a burden on their monthly budget or, in some cases, rethinking exactly how much they want to leave behind. If maintaining a life insurance policy is coming at the expense of your comfort and ability to live the life you want in retirement, is it really worth the extra payout for your heirs who are, in most cases, financially solvent adults? It's easy to become so focused on legacy planning that we forget to account for our own needs and wants.

Another area in which people often worry is in dealing with health care costs in retirement. Many people don't realize how comprehensive Medicare is once you reach age sixty-five. If you purchase a modest supplemental plan, you can protect yourself against most health expenses. Clearly there are one-off cases where out-of-pocket costs are high, but for the most part, Medicare and supplemental insurance cover them. Barring something truly strange and catastrophic, that simple and affordable setup will cover the majority of your costs. My parents have been on Medicare for decades and have been through multiple health issues, including knee replacements and cancer surgeries. In the end the out-of-pocket costs for these items were more than manageable. While people tend to overestimate their future medical expenses once they are on Medicare, they correspondingly tend to underestimate their need for long-term care; possibly this is because people think of long-term care as part and parcel with general medical care or possibly because people don't like to think about needing help for daily tasks. Nevertheless, long-term care is something that every retiree needs to think seriously about. I'll cover this topic more thoroughly in the next chapter, but in-home or residential care is something that almost everyone has to face if they live—as we all hope to do—to an advanced age. For a married couple, the odds that at least one of them will require some sort of specialized care is very good. Long-term care is not covered by Medicare, so dealing with that potential expense is each person's own responsibility.

Similarly, many people don't accurately estimate the levels of risk they are exposed to via their investment assets. For example, some retirees maintain rental properties as a way of supplementing their income. Very few of them would consider themselves to be in the real estate business, and they often see these ventures as a way to bring in money with relatively little effort on their part. Because it was never seen as their primary "career" or even a "real" business, many of these assets are not structured properly to protect against litigation risk and often leave the owner open to potentially losing way more than they offer.

Renting out a property carries certain legal responsibilities that people don't always fully understand, and the consequences for that misunderstanding can be expensive. If someone is injured or suffers damage in or as a result of living in your property, you can be held responsible for that and may have to make financial recompense to the injured person. If you simply own the property as a private person with no additional legal framework, a good portion of your personal assets could be on the table in a potential suit. The solution to this is relatively simple: put any rental properties in an LLC (limited liability corporation). Just as the name implies, LLCs protect you by restricting the financial responsibility to only what is inside the LLC. Thus, if someone gets hurt on your rental property, they can't sue you as Joe Smith, random individual, and take a settlement from any of your personal assets; they can only sue Joe Smith's Rental House, LLC, which only contains the value of the property itself. Forming this kind of LLC is absolutely a type of "insurance," though it's rarely what people imagine when they hear that word.

I mentioned previously that many people use life insurance as a form of catastrophic financial planning, and while that can be done in more or less advantageous ways, it is a legitimate and useful tool for transferring wealth. The key to using insurance in this way is timing. Timing, in general, is the bedrock principle of insurance. By its very nature, you need to have your insurance in place before X negative thing happens, and when you get into more complex issues of how to get the most out of a product, *when* you purchase matters as much as *what* you purchase.

> Timing, in general, is the bedrock principle of insurance.

Certain types of insurance policies can act as investment vehicles, and if you own them for the right amount of time, you can take advantage of most of the positive features while sidestepping the problem of becoming overinsured or incorrectly insured. For example, we had a situation a few years ago where a client came to me and said, "I want to put $20,000 a year in an account for my grandkids. I don't need it. I want you to manage it." That is always something a financial advisor likes to hear, but before we put that money into a traditional investment vehicle, I wanted to explore a couple of other options.

I looked at the client's financial situation and did some independent research, and I discovered that, for $20,000 per year, we could purchase a "second-to-die" policy. This is essentially a life insurance policy that "skips" the traditional beneficiary (one's spouse) and only pays out after both partners have passed away. It's a good tool for transferring wealth because it offers more or less the same value you'd get from buying two life insurance policies at a much lower premium. In my client's case, I was able to get about $1.1 million for his $20,000 per year.

It was at this point that the issue of timing came in. The reason these policies are generally less expensive is because both parties have to pass away before the disbursement happens, which, in theory, should allow the insurance company to collect premiums for a longer period of time. As with most life insurance policies, the longer you pay premiums, the less valuable the eventual payout will be. If you're paying $20,000 a year for fifty years, for example, then the insurance company will have actually collected the majority of that $1.1 million from you already. That's another reason this type of product is better for legacy planning: there's not much danger you're going to keep paying for another fifty years.

Still, we had to determine exactly when this policy would cease to be a better alternative to other forms of investment. We ran something called an "internal rate of return," which tells us what kind of return we are getting on that money in any given year. For example, if my client and his wife had both passed away one year after buying the policy, they would receive $1.1 million dollars for their $20,000 investment, making it probably the best investment they'd ever made. If that happened in two years, the internal rate of return is slightly less phenomenal, as they'd now have $40,000 in their investment and so on and so forth, until we reached the point where it would be more beneficial to have some other kind of product. We eventually found that, at about twenty-five years out, we would still have to be getting between 6 and 7 percent returns every year on an investment to match the life insurance's rate of return. Critically, that $1.1 million from the life insurance policy is also guaranteed, something that you can't say about most other forms of investment. Even if you did manage to get 7 percent returns for the life of your other investment, you could still happen to pass away at a bad time in the market and substantially decrease your intended bequest.

There's a little bit of "financial chicken" involved in this kind of planning, where we make educated guesses about a person's likely life span and proceed from there. If a client in their early fifties with a spouse twenty years their junior came to me with this same issue, I would certainly not advise them to purchase a policy that likely wouldn't pay out for three or four decades. For a couple in their late seventies or early eighties, however, the math is much more favorable.

Successfully insuring yourself is more than just buying any one product; it's about assessing a complex situation, identifying the most urgent risks, and having the depth of knowledge necessary to address those risks with the best possible solutions. It's about having the right type and amount of coverage at the right time and being able to adapt your strategy through all the stages of the economic life cycle. I sometimes think of it as a bit like a game of Tetris: you have to very quickly assess where the gaps are and fit the right pieces into them, all while making sure you mitigate risk from multiple other sources. If you aren't paying close attention, risk piles up rapidly, and pretty soon, it's game over.

CHAPTER ELEVEN

LONG-TERM CARE

People often avoid talking about or addressing the problems of insurance because they find the topic too unpleasant, but if you press them about it, they will, like my road-biking buddy, acknowledge that it's something they need to think about. When it comes to the issue of long-term care, however, a great many of us don't even realize it's a topic they should be considering at all. We all (with a very few unusual exceptions) accept our mortality on some level—no one really expects to live forever—but a lot of people do behave as though they are going to remain more or less healthy and independent up until their death. Unfortunately, statistics tell us that's not the case.

"Long-term care" is an umbrella term that covers everything from residency in a facility to hiring someone to do laundry or get groceries a few times per week. What it's not is "acute care," which is provided during the treatment of a health problem. So if you spend a few nights in the hospital after a heart attack, that's acute care. If you subsequently have a nurse come to your house to help you with daily tasks you can no longer handle due to your heart attack, that is long-term care. Many people head into retirement very concerned about the former and far less aware of the latter.

As I've mentioned before, it's not the acute care that is the big money drain in retirement. Medicare and private insurance defray most of the largest expenses. Instead, it's the steady drumbeat of a significant monthly expense that often was not anticipated that can really derail retirement plans. People hear about a surgical procedure or a treatment that costs hundreds of thousands, and they, quite reasonably, worry about how they would manage if something like that happened to them. We don't hear nearly as much about the cost of assisted living or other long-term medical expenses, which may seem like more modest costs but build up over the months and years. Oftentimes, those costs are actually not that modest at all. One of my partners here at Watermark Wealth Strategies had a grandfather who recently passed away. The man spent the last five years of his life in a memory care facility, and that stay alone cost nearly half a million dollars. It wasn't a particularly posh or elite facility, either, simply a place where he could get the kind of care and oversight he needed because of his advanced dementia.

It is particularly difficult to estimate the true cost of long-term care overall because a lot of it is actually done outside of the formal medical system. By far the single biggest source of long-term care overall is still relatives, and many people who don't have a specific plan for this element of their lives often assume that they will address the problem in that way. It's easy to see why people think that way; it's an ancient model of care. Almost every human society has some cultural expectation that children will care for their elderly parents, but modern American life has made this an unreliable option at best, and, at worst, completely unworkable on the large scale.

For one thing, we are living longer on average than ever before. Conditions associated with advanced age like Alzheimer's or extreme frailty are on the rise, not because they've actually become more common but because a greater number of people are living long enough to become vulnerable to them. This means more people requiring more specialized care for longer. Additionally, our economic and social life cycles are changing, and more and more of the younger generations are delaying marriage or children and may take longer to establish traditional careers. This means that, by the time their parents are in need of care, they might not be in a position economically or logistically to provide that. It's so common a problem that there's an actual term for it: the "sandwich generation," for those who are struggling to care for aged parents as well as their own young children.

Just because someone loves you, that doesn't mean they are equipped to provide medical care for you.

The biggest problem with this way of doing things, however, is the simple fact that just because someone loves you, that doesn't mean they are equipped to provide medical care for you. Most of the people who provide this kind of care don't have the professional background they'd really need to help someone struggling with a complex disease, and, critically, they don't have the emotional and mental health resources that a professional would have either. Caregiving can be extremely taxing physically and mentally, and when you are caring for a loved one, you are often "on the clock" virtually all of the time. It can and does take a serious toll on the caregiver's health as well.

This is one big reason that I push back whenever someone suggests that they can look after their partner (or vice versa) by themselves. In fact, I usually have them do a little exercise to illustrate the point:

have your spouse lie on the ground, and then try to pick them up. When they inevitably can't lift or move them more than an inch or two, I point out that, if their spouse were physically incapacitated, they literally could not help them. This problem is compounded by the fact that women more commonly end up in caretaker roles, and they may suddenly have to face the challenge of helping their 250-pound husbands in and out of the shower every day. Even if there's not a huge disparity between the sizes of the two people, we often underestimate how hard it is to lift or manipulate someone who is truly dead weight.

More than any issue of physics, however, is the question of what sort of experiences we want to have with our loved ones. Do you really want your last years with a spouse or child to be filled with that kind of stress, fatigue, and frustration? Do you want to damage the health of your husband or wife and hasten their own decline? Do you want to put a heavy financial and personal burden on your children? Most people instinctively do not want that, and while people are drawn to the comfort and familiarity of having family take care of them, most people would probably prefer to get medical attention from someone who knows what they need and how best to provide it. It's a sobering idea, but when we're really honest with ourselves, it's easy to see which option is superior. A big part of the reason the family caregiving model persists is simply that people don't have the resources to do anything else, often because they didn't plan for it at all.

The other common answer that I get to this line of questioning is an almost off-the-cuff insistence that the client doesn't need to think about long-term care because they'd rather go out in a blaze of glory first. It's a pretty understandable reaction—it's almost impossible to imagine ourselves in that kind of scenario, so we instead default to a future where we just don't let it happen. It reminds me somewhat of the way children or young adults will talk about "when they are grown up" and all the things they will never do or be. How many times did we vow never to do *X* thing when we became a mom or dad, only to turn around and embrace it with our own kids? Who among us hasn't made a choice that would have shocked their younger self?

It's a normal, natural part of growing older, and discovering that the situation is just a whole lot different when you're actually in it. I will say, I've talked to a lot of people who said some variation of "I won't let that happen to me," but typically a person facing long-term care actually doesn't have many options.

> Long-term care can take many forms, and we don't always have to default to the worst possible situation.

In addition to realizing that kind of thinking is almost certainly more fantasy than reality, it also helps to realize that long-term care can take many forms, and we don't always have to default to the worst possible situation. You could very well live happily to be ninety-eight years old and need someone to help out around the house a few times per week, and that still counts as long-term care and still requires financial planning. Even a residential facility, which is probably the first and most dire outcome people imagine when they think about this topic, doesn't necessarily mean your life will be miserable. Different places exist to serve different needs, from people who are mostly independent but benefit from the structure and availability of a staff, to people with specific health problems that make it unsafe for them to stay in their home. The goal is to keep you safe and comfortable, and while it's true that there are bad facilities and bad caregivers, the better you plan and the more carefully you structure your assets, the more options will be available to you.

Once we accept that the need for long-term care in retirement is a real risk, then we can start talking about how to resolve this problem. There are essentially three ways to go:

1. You self-insure. This is probably the simplest way to manage the situation. If something happens, you just plan to pay out of pocket. Obviously, this is really only feasible for people who have the money to account for any curveballs life might throw at them. In general, a couple probably needs $4 million to $5 million minimum in investments to comfortably self-insure the both of them in this way.

    The biggest risk with this option is the pocketbook pinch. Long-term care is not like acute care, where a medical procedure or a hospital stay will cost you pretty much the same anywhere you go in the United States. It's true that people sometimes do pursue rarer or more experimental treatments that have additional costs, but in general, no one is comparison shopping for a triple bypass. Long-term care, by contrast, is highly variable, and you will often pay more for more services and higher quality. When it comes to the health and comfort of your spouse, obviously you want to give them everything you can. No one wants to find themselves in a position where they have to choose a person or place to care for their loved one based not on quality but rather on which one fits in your budget.

    If you do choose to allocate more money for a better facility or service, you then face the issue of how to live on what is left of your monthly budget. A good residential facility can easily cost up to $100,000 per year in some parts of the country, and that's all money you weren't expecting to spend every month. How can you ensure not only that your spouse's needs are met but that you can also survive comfortably? This is one of the major reasons we don't do option 1 very often. Even if a client has the means to do it, it's almost always better for them to transfer some of that risk to an insurance company.

2. Traditional long-term-care insurance. This works much like life insurance, with one important caveat: you buy it and pay your yearly premiums, and if you go into long-term care, the policy disburses and covers part or all of the costs. Unlike a traditional life insurance policy, however, if you don't end up needing long-term care, the policy simply closes, and the insurance company keeps the premiums you have paid over the life of the policy. That's a frustrating idea for a lot of people who, naturally, don't want to spend years paying into something that never materially benefits them. Additionally, it's increasingly difficult for insurance companies to accurately price these policies, especially as the long-term-care market shifts over time. Most people are subject to constantly rising premiums as they get older, which can start to make the whole enterprise feel like it's costing you more than it offers.

My eighty-seven-year-old father has this type of insurance, and last year's premium was $7,800, which is a considerable amount of money. It's enough money that you have to pause and really ask yourself what to do next: Do you write a check for $7,800, or do you not write a check for $7,800? If you stop, now he has no long-term care insurance, and it's not as though you get anything back from years of paying premiums. Plus, he's now at a point in his life when he's more likely than ever to actually need that coverage, which is exactly why those premiums are so high. So you grudgingly write that check for $7,800 and hope he doesn't use it. Next year, it might be $800 more, and the next year it might be $500 more, and you will need to constantly make that calculation of whether the security is worth the financial cost.

3. A hybrid plan. This is a new idea that we've seen a lot of success with. Basically, it's a combination of options 1 and 2, where you simply allocate a certain dollar amount of your net worth toward covering your long-term care. In most cases, we usually end up using between $40,000 and $50,000 per person, and we buy a policy that gives us a pool of assets that we can tap into. That pool of assets grows, so though you may buy the policy at sixty-five, when you have a small chance of actually needing it, if you hold on to it for twenty years at a 3 percent or 4 percent inflation rate, that's quite a bit of growth. If you do need it, you can access a certain dollar amount for your care or your spouse's care. If you end up not using it and you die, then your heirs get the original cost of the policy back.

For example, if you bought a $50,000 long-term care policy, it's going to have a pool of money that might be anywhere from $120,000 to $170,000 the day you start. Typically, you are able to get double or triple your original investment when you buy the policy, and that money is going to continue to grow, which means you'll have even more flexibility if you do need it. If you don't use it, or only use part of it, the remaining value of the original investment will still go to your heirs. So in this example, your spouse or children would get that $50,000 to use for whatever they might need after your passing. Clients tend to prefer this option because it doesn't have that frustrating emotional component of paying into something without knowing if it's ever actually going to do anything for you.

The idea of planning (financially and otherwise) for this kind of medical care is an unsettling concept, so I don't blame people for overlooking it or even resisting the idea. If you think about it, however, it just represents an advancement in our ability to provide for people as a society. There was once a time when it wouldn't have necessarily occurred to anyone that they needed to have some sort of way to financially provide for their families in the event of their deaths. Instead, it would have been assumed that extended family would cover the gap, no matter how difficult or unworkable that solution might have been. It wasn't until insurance existed as a concept that people could really begin to think beyond a simple dependence on kinship ties and decide what would actually give their family the best possible protection.

It may be a little grim to think about, but planning for these sorts of eventualities is a way of taking the reins in your own life, rather than simply reacting to whatever happens. Being sick, needing help, needing long-term care—these are scary concepts, but they pale before the idea of needing all those things and not knowing how to get them. The difference between the two is the difference between making a perilous climb down a mountain and falling off one.

Chapter Twelve

ESTATE PLANNING

One might imagine that it's a whole lot easier to get people on board with estate planning than it is to encourage them to delve into the topics of the last two chapters, and to a certain degree, that's true. People are more interested in discussing their legacy than pondering the end of their lives. Most people also like the idea of leaving something behind for those they love and want to make their wishes on that subject understood. The difficulty comes from how opaque the whole legacy process can be and the preconceived notions clients have about it. More often than not, when I raise the subject of estate planning with a client, I just get a deer-in-the-headlights stare because it's not something they thought they'd really need to consider. In reality, estate planning isn't a niche add-on; it's the cornerstone of a solid financial plan.

The two biggest preconceptions people have about estate planning are:

1) It's very complicated, and

2) It's only for the extremely wealthy.

These two ideas are interrelated and arise from a misunderstanding about the purpose of estate planning. Many people think that estate planning is designed to avoid some of the tax bite of wealth transfer, specifically estate tax. At the time of this writing, a married couple can pass north of $22 million to their heirs without triggering an estate tax, which is much more than the vast majority of people are intending to bequeath. So people hear that number and think, "Why should I worry about a complex tax structure when my smaller estate doesn't have to face those problems?"

It's sound reasoning, but it's coming from a faulty premise. Estate planning is not intended just to deal with taxes, nor with any one part of the financial process. Estate planning exists to help you transfer assets to your heirs in the best possible way. Yes, sometimes that means figuring out tax issues, but more commonly, it means assessing your entire situation and finding a way to ensure that your wishes are actually carried out with the effects that you intended. That is a service that anyone who wants to leave something for their heirs' needs, whether it's $22 million or $22,000.

Along with the misperception of estate planning as a service for people who have large amounts of assets in various forms, people also mistakenly think that something like a trust is overkill for their comparatively straightforward portfolio. Most people also tend to place a lot of responsibility on their families and other heirs to do the work of managing an estate. This isn't always a conscious decision; most people simply assume that many of their intentions will be obvious and noncontroversial, so it won't be very difficult to sort things out after they are gone. People believe that if they write down these straightforward intentions in a will, that will be sufficient to ensure that all of their assets are properly allocated. That is probably the most unfortunate misconception about estate planning: people do not realize the risks and limitations of a typical will.

The first thing you have to know about a will is that it's not a legacy silver bullet. More than a century of popular culture has led us to believe that wills are almost like holy scripts—what the will says is what happens, period. In reality, every will is going to go through probate court. Remember this: a will *will* go through probate! There, it will be verified and details ironed out, clarifications made, and errors or omissions addressed. As with most other court proceedings, the probate process makes your will essentially public, with details and documents available to anyone who requests them. Also, like any other court process, this usually takes a while (sometimes a very long while), and there will be associated fees. The average cost of probate is 1 to 2 percent of the total assets of the estate, and the whole thing can take anywhere from nine months to upward of ten years.

Yes, I said years. A flawed or contested will can drag out for more than a decade, with fees steadily draining the estate itself the whole time. On a certain level, this shouldn't be a huge surprise. When you throw yourself into the court system—possibly the biggest red-tape generator in American life—of course it's going to eat up time and money. Unfortunately, this often has the exact opposite effect than what someone intended when they wrote their will: it puts more barriers between their heirs and their intended bequests. It can also add stress and stoke resentments between family members, especially if the will is unclear or incomplete in any way. Many wills are incomplete because people either go too general ("my son and daughter each get 50 percent") or focus on the specific assets they want to pass along and forget about things like houses and cars, which also have to go through probate.

I recently had a client who experienced the probate process firsthand when his brother-in-law passed away. He had to fly with his wife all the way to Kansas, where the will was going through court, and his wife had to get a local lawyer to manage her part of the process. They wound up staying for about six weeks and spent considerable amounts both on the legal proceedings themselves and the costs of relocating for more than a month. In the end, they managed to sort the situation out in a way that was satisfactory but not ideal. They wound up with a tax setup that neither of them favored and were left wondering why it had to be so hard. I am sure that wasn't his brother-in-law's intention when he left a portion of his estate for his sister with no real planning done.

A living trust is far superior in every way to a traditional will, and it's the option that I favor in most cases. Even though the very name tends to conjure up images of generational wealth or idle rich kids, a trust is truly a wide-ranging tool that is applicable to many people, especially those approaching retirement. In addition to being more flexible and more precise, trusts provide additional protection and control over one's assets . Essentially, a trust is a documented legal agreement between three people: the original asset holder who initiates the trust, a "trustee" who is authorized to hold those assets and distribute them to the third party, and that third party, the beneficiary. When you are alive, you may play all three roles. A trust bypasses the problem of probate by assigning one party to interpret and carry out your documented wishes. All of this can be done without going through probate. The appointment of a trustee also means that if something does happen to you and you require a person to represent your interests or manage your financial affairs, that person is already designated and in place. With a traditional will, time is often frittered away deciding upon who should take point and getting them in the legal position to do so.

People often overlook trusts as an option because they assume that trusts are very difficult to set up and administer. Possibly because they are culturally associated with large, complex wealth holdings, it's assumed that the documents themselves are extremely complex, and setting one up is much like the legal version of defusing a bomb. Wills, by contrast, appear straightforward. Don't you just write down what you want to happen? While that is technically true, it is in the interpretation and administration of those "wants" that thorny legal questions start to become a problem.

Unfortunately, trusts have somewhat earned their reputation as challenging to prepare, but that is largely a side effect of the law firms that create them having a personal interest in making the process lengthy and difficult. After all, they do bill hourly. This isn't to say that all law firms are needlessly complicating their trusts, but it is a problem in the industry. A trust document doesn't have to be dense with legalese to be sound and useful, however, and I have found that making the trust as straightforward as possible also helps to keep it adaptable and useful.

At Watermark Wealth Strategies, we use a trust we call a Dynasty Trust because it is designed to serve generations of our clients. A good trust can last for five hundred years, provided there's still money in it. To get that kind of longevity, though, we made sure that our trust was easy to understand and to change. Not only does the language need to be open enough to let us make those changes as needed, but the document itself also has to be comprehensible to the client so that they understand when they need to come to us and request some alteration. If you don't really understand what your trust does and how it works, you could unknowingly be putting yourself at risk.

One of the things we do for new clients is review their existing retirement and legacy plans, including any trusts they might have in place. I would say approximately 40 percent of the time, the trusts aren't doing what the client wants them to do and believes them to be doing. Part of it is down to the array in the quality of these documents. As with a will, you don't need special licensure to write a trust; technically, if you wanted to print a template off the internet and fill in the blanks, you could create your own trust at home, though that doesn't typically work out very well for most people. The other problem is that people don't update their trusts when relevant circumstances change in their lives, often because they didn't fully understand the provisions of the trust in the first place. Similarly, I see a lot of trusts that aren't much better than wills because they are written in such a way that they skipped over a lot of the most important features of a trust or they are not enacted until after probate.

One big example is the structure of the payout. There are a lot of trusts that simply kick the money free at some end date (usually when the beneficiary turns twenty-one), and all those assets are put in the beneficiary's name. The point of a trust, however, is to protect your assets, and the moment they leave the trust, those protections are gone. What you want is a trust that allows the beneficiary access at a certain point, which allows them to use that money without exposing it to all the risks associated with any other account. Having a trust that pays out and then dissolves is a bit like putting your cell phone in a waterproof case and then popping it out to take some cool underwater photos. Why would you buy a protective shell only to throw it away at the riskiest moment?

I think these types of trusts are so common for two reasons. Firstly, the people drawing up these trusts have a simple goal of getting their client's estate through probate. They aren't focused on long-term protection of the assets, just on making sure the client's wishes aren't litigated for years on end. From their perspective, it doesn't matter what happens to money after it disburses. And clients don't challenge this for the second reason: most people don't fully understand what a trust can do. If a client can't parse the language of the trust and doesn't have the specific financial literacy necessary to know all the options available, they are forced to trust the judgment of whoever is preparing the trust for them. That's why we go out of our way to make sure that the client is fully informed about all the provisions and possibilities with our trust. The average person could read our Dynasty Trust and understand at least 90 percent of it immediately, and the rest we are ready to explain when we go over the details in person.

In addition to the language of the document being straightforward, the actual creation of the trust is a quick and streamlined process as well. The biggest investment of time is up front, when we ask you roughly fifteen or so questions about your life, your family, and your wishes. This generally takes about forty-five minutes to an hour but can go longer, depending on how complicated someone's situation is (or how gregarious they may be). After that, your part in the process is largely complete. We use the information you give us to draw up a personalized version of the trust that covers all your bases and can go into effect immediately.

There are some important logistical questions on our trust interview, things like whether you'd like to donate your organs and whom you want to designate as your healthcare power of attorney, but the things that are dwelled upon the most in those interviews are the interpersonal issues. For many people, that is the most challenging part of the process, as these are things most people don't dwell on very often in their regular life. This is true for any comprehensive legacy planning, however, and avoiding those sometimes tough conversations is tempting but shortsighted. Failing to plan for potential problems usually just means leaving your loved ones to sort out a messy situation without your help or advice.

One of the great benefits of legacy planning is that it can force us to really think about the impact of wealth and how we can use our wealth in the best way to give our loved ones the best possible life. The precision and certainty of the trust is a great asset when it comes to thinking through possible problems and developing solutions. A trust is also the best way to put "guardrails" on the assets you leave behind. Not only is there an actual person mediating between the estate and the beneficiaries, but the trust itself also offers more options for customizing an inheritance. For example, some of our clients have younger children, so we build those trusts to ensure that there is life insurance and there are appropriate assets available to keep their kids safe and comfortable until they reach adulthood. But what then? Do we just dump the remainder of the estate on the child the moment they turn eighteen? If you don't have the right structures in place, that's exactly what happens.

The default legal process is that a person inherits upon reaching the age of majority which, in most states, is eighteen. Those who have ever been—or been near—an eighteen-year-old, however, know very well that it is not the age of maturity. At least, not for most of us. Even intelligent, level-headed people much older than eighteen have a lot of trouble dealing with a large influx of new assets. Statistically, if you were to give a large lump sum of money to any person who is not mentally ready for it, they would fritter it away inside of eighteen months on average. The problem goes deeper than a simple waste of money, however: putting the burden of wealth (and, yes, it absolutely can be a burden) on a young person who isn't ready for it can actively harm their development into a successful adult.

Many of my clients are largely self-made. Whatever assets they've amassed weren't built on any significant inheritance, and most of them are very proud of their success and the hard work they've done to earn it. When I'm talking to them about this issue, I often give them this hypothetical: imagine that, instead of spending years you spent working and striving and failing and recovering and learning all those hard lessons, some time traveler went back to your eighteenth birthday and handed you everything you have now. How successful do you imagine you would be? And not just in your industry either—how well equipped would you be to manage adult life?

Immediately having access to a large pool of assets as you enter adulthood is not the norm. Instead of entering the workforce and learning how to manage your finances in the way most of us do, someone with a trust that triggers on their eighteenth birthday instead gets a short period of no-consequences spending followed by an inevitable ugly crash back down to earth. If that person is lucky, it really is just a short period, and they can start over without too much trouble. If they are less fortunate, they may have missed invaluable opportunities to cultivate vital skills and traits and, in exchange, have developed bad financial habits that will haunt the rest of their lives.

At the same time, most people don't want to wait until their heirs are sober, middle-aged people who have already addressed most of their major life expenses before allowing them to benefit from their parents' estate at all. Most people want the money they leave behind to function much as it would have had they been there to share it in person. Most people want to help their children establish themselves and give them opportunities to do things like pursue an education, purchase a home, or start a family of their own. A trust allows us to get extremely granular about when and how much of the estate is dispersed to the heirs. You could, for example, control the money, using a nonchild trustee until your child reached the age of twenty-five, but still make an exception for educational expenses like tuition and housing. You could stagger access to the various assets so your child has a chance to learn and make mistakes with a small amount of money while still protecting the bulk of your estate.

Most people contemplating retirement, however, have children who are adults (or almost adults), and for them, the question is less about when it is generally the most useful to give someone money and more about the individuals involved. This is where people have to make an honest assessment of the people they love and determine what would actually help them and what might hurt them. If you know, for example, that one of your children struggles with addiction, giving them a lump sum could be very destructive to them. In that case, you might need to develop a plan where the trustee plays a more active role in approving expenses to ensure that while your child has access to the things they need, they don't have the temptation of a blank check. Or maybe you feel like your money can't benefit that child at all anymore, and instead, you would like to provide for his or her children. We can create a trust with a generation-skipping ability that allows you to bypass traditional next of kin and preserve the estate for others.

Even in a less dire situation, there are lots of reasons you might want a more customized trust. Many of my clients have blended families with lots of children, stepchildren, and multiple sets of parents in the mix. There are a lot of variables at play here, including the assets of the husband and wife, both separate and shared, as well as the relationships between all parties and any existing plans that are in place to provide for the family in the event of a death. In a lot of cases, especially if the couple married later in life and their children were older when they met, the husband and wife would prefer that their individual assets go to their biological children. That kind of thing is a lot easier to do in a trust than in the weaker framework of a will.

The most important thing is to think about your potential heirs as human beings. Who is good with money? Who isn't? Who needs the most support? Who would use it as a crutch? We often think of inheritance in terms of simple "fairness" and splitting everything equally, but the happiness and security of your loved ones isn't a geometry problem, and it can't be solved by simply divvying everything up in the most direct way. Instead of thinking of an inheritance as a measure of how much someone is loved or a "reward" for being related to you, think about it as a powerful and potentially dangerous tool. Giving someone money is like giving them gunpowder: with the right materials and the right precautionary measures, they might make some beautiful fireworks with it. Without those tools and those safety mechanisms, they could cripple themselves for life.

Even if all your potential heirs are responsible and financially astute, a trust can still play an important role in protecting assets from things outside the control of you or your heirs. For example, assets in a trust can be made "divorce-proof," meaning they do not count as shared property for the purposes of designating who gets what in a divorce. Most people, even if they like their son- or daughter-in-law, would not like the idea of that person having a portion of their estate, but that's exactly what would happen with a typical will. The problem with a will is that there's no structure to the assets once someone has inherited them; it's simply a matter of what that person chooses to do with them. Most people treat it like any other income and put it in checking or savings, but once it becomes commingled with all the other household assets, there's no way to sift it out again at a later date. If a trust is already in place, it's much easier simply to let it stay there, where it has all sorts of protections. In the event that someone's marital status does change, that money is completely quarantined and separate from the rest of the couple's assets, and all your heir needs to do is remove their former spouse's name from the list of beneficiaries.

Furthermore, a trust can also make these assets judgment- and creditor-proof. This means that even if your heir has to declare bankruptcy for some reason, the assets inside the trust cannot be assessed by the bankruptcy court. It doesn't matter the size of the outstanding debt or of the protected assets; if it's in the trust, creditors can't come after it. Similarly, "judgment-proof" means that this money can't be taken in any sort of litigation. So if your heir is sued and held responsible, the assets in the trust cannot be seized to pay any fees or restitution. These fail-safes are a big part of why I say that a good trust can last five centuries—it's impossible to eliminate every financial risk in the world, but these protections combine to insulate you from a large percentage of them.

Finally, a good trust package also allows you to bundle up several other important provisions, including financial and medical power of attorney and a living will. The power-of-attorney element is particularly important because a lot of people have a big vulnerability there that they likely don't even know about. It would seem obvious that, if one partner is rendered indisposed by some sort of medical problem, their spouse would automatically have control over their finances. In reality, it's more complicated than that.

While a spouse would have access to most shared accounts, if we're talking about something like an IRA or any other qualified account, no one other than the account holder can get access without a financial power of attorney. This is particularly a problem for people in retirement because a lot of retirement funds are in qualified accounts, and it's very likely that major expenses would need to be paid out of those accounts.

I actually saw this scenario happen to a relatively new client of ours, a couple who was looking to optimize their existing retirement plan. We hadn't finished setting up their legacy planning when the husband, Tom, went into the hospital and unfortunately fell into a coma. His wife, Sharon, called us, frantic. In addition to the stress of Tom's illness, she had a large looming house payment, and she needed access to his IRA to pay the bill. Unfortunately, because there was no durable power of attorney in their case, we could not legally take money from Tom's account for anyone except Tom. With Tom comatose and unable to consent to any legal agreements, the only thing she could do was take the issue to court and hope to be made a conservator for her husband. Unfortunately, that's yet another protracted legal process that can take months and, in some cases, can cost you a lot in legal fees.

Sharon was able to get a conservatorship for Tom, and we helped her organize her other assets to cover her bills in the meantime, but having financial power of attorney in place would have saved her so much time and stress. When you are in a heightened emotional situation where you are worried about the health of a loved one, the last things you need are more complications and more logistical problems to solve. Having a comprehensive trust provides a safety net for those common scenarios.

I mentioned before that a will is not a legacy silver bullet, and I am not claiming that a trust is that either. In truth, there's no silver bullet for legacy planning because each person, family, and situation is different. A trust is more like a very good legacy multitool. It won't solve every problem you encounter, but it does give you a lot of options for facing those problems. The flexible and expansive nature of the trust particularly appeals to me because I also think it embodies Watermark's approach to financial management in general and estate planning in particular. Legacy planning is all about thinking beyond the immediate moment and imagining a future for the people we love. To do this kind of preparation properly, you can't work on such a small scale. Appropriately, we at Watermark Wealth Strategies are not aiming for short-range goals like simply getting your money from A to B without going through probate; we are here to help you complete your entire journey, whether you want that journey to last five years or five hundred.

CHAPTER THIRTEEN

HOLISTIC PLANNING

When I began this book, I talked about how financial advisors play a Sherpa-like role for our clients. There is, however, one important way in which we differ (and I don't mean our relative levels of cardio fitness): a Sherpa usually doesn't show up until you actually get to the mountain, and the mountain is, in many ways, only a small part of the climber's journey. "Climbing Mount Everest" doesn't begin at base camp, nor even on the plane to Nepal. People spend years preparing for that kind of challenge; for many, it is the culmination of a lifetime of training. Over the course of that lifetime, there were probably lots of people who provided advice, education, or even just companionship, and without those people, the individual may never have even made it to the mountain, let alone completed their climb. My goal—and the goal of Watermark Wealth Strategies overall—is to provide a service that encompasses all of those important assistants whose contributions allowed the climber to conquer some new element of their quest.

Perhaps because I recently remodeled my house, I can't help but think about the kind of planning we offer clients as similar to the work that a general contractor does. In theory, you could have individual working relationships with your plumber, your electrician, your contractor, and any other specialists you might require, but it's a whole lot easier if there's one person who manages all of those "departments." That way, you can offload the mental work of ensuring that all elements of the project aren't just going well on their own but are also fitting into the plan for the completed work as a whole.

While this is common practice in the construction industry, financial planners haven't really embraced this model the way they should. Managing your money over the course of a lifetime is one of the most complex projects we will ever undertake, and as we've seen in this book, there are a lot of discrete elements involved that require expertise. Your tax guy shouldn't be handling your trust fund in the same way that your drywall expert probably shouldn't also install your heating and cooling system. Yet most firms are specialized, and there's no guarantee that they will communicate—or even attempt to communicate—with any other specialized professionals a client may also employ. Traditionally, clients have just had to hope that their estate firm talks to their tax preparer and so forth and that no one is working at cross-purposes. It is presumed that because everyone has general knowledge of finance, they won't make any significant oversights with their part of the project. To return to the contractor analogy, this is like never having any of the team members talk to each other because you figure they all know what houses look like, so they can't screw it up too badly. Having a team where the individual members don't communicate and may not all participate in crafting the overall strategy is a recipe for inefficiency and mistakes—that's how you wind up with a toilet in what was supposed to be your kitchen.

When Watermark Wealth Strategies was established, we knew we wanted to do something different and correct what was, to us, an obvious blind spot in the industry. Since then, our clients have consistently praised the comprehensive nature of our services. It gives them peace of mind knowing that we are accounting for all dimensions of their financial plan and that they are saved the effort of juggling a whole suite of professionals. We are able to do this because we've made a concerted effort to broaden our expertise, both by educating ourselves and by hiring on people with the specific expertise and skills we may be missing. Even more importantly, however, we can provide holistic planning because

> **We can provide holistic planning because we start every new client relationship by nailing down their overall vision.**

we start every new client relationship by nailing down their overall vision. After all, the best contractor in the world still can't build the right house without an architect and a plan.

Our initial meetings with clients are designed not so much to take stock of their financial situation but to answer one question above all else: When you think about your future, what do you see? To get to that answer, we usually ask a lot of smaller questions about the kinds of topics covered in this book. We dig into what people plan to do with their time in retirement, whether they want to travel or buy a new house or move to Belize, and how they want to provide for their heirs. For each of these big questions, I usually have several smaller questions that are designed to really flesh out the client's thinking. As I've mentioned before, people typically have a very general sense of what they want to do in retirement, and it's usually just the big-picture stuff. It's my job to help them think in terms of their day-to-day experiences. Often, this process involves so much background on their lives, their preferences, and their dreams that clients joke as they leave that I know more about them than many of their family members do.

I consider these preliminary interviews to be the most important part of the process, and it often surprises people that we don't necessarily ask them to bring any financial documents with them. The financial element is important, of course, and many people do come to a first meeting with financials in hand, but that information is sort of like the actual building materials. Yes, a contractor needs to know how much lumber to buy or what kind of windows to install, but none of that helps if he or she doesn't know what kind of building he is supposed to construct. Developing a plan for someone's retirement isn't about numbers; it's about understanding people and what they need as people. I like to say that it's not so much financial coaching but life coaching, and it's my job to make sure that you get the best possible "return" on your working life thus far.

> Developing a plan for someone's retirement isn't about numbers; it's about understanding people and what they need as people.

People have a tendency to let money take the reins in their life. It's not necessarily about a fixation on wealth (though that can be a problem) but rather that people are conditioned to look at the bottom line and decide, based on that, what to do. After a lifetime of making decisions that way, it's sometimes hard for people to talk about their future choices without doing the math as they go. That's why I like to get into the finer details of lifestyle and relationships and purpose— it allows people to think outside of simple resource management and really start to consider what makes them happy and what doesn't.

This approach also helps us provide what I think is one of our most important services: general troubleshooting. Because we cover the full spectrum of financial services and because we take the time to learn about each client's needs and intentions in detail, we are prepared to resolve just about any issue that might come up in retirement. From utilizing Medicare to buying a car, we can adapt our plans to accommodate just about any need or want. Other firms that don't have the same breadth of expertise are often less flexible in their planning. Specializing in one element or another forces them to think primarily in terms of whatever they already understand, rather than being able to build a plan organically that can grow and change with the individual.

As a firm, we don't have any particular stake in the mechanics of your retirement plan. A good contractor doesn't insist you have to build a ranch-style home if you really want a Tudor, and a good Sherpa doesn't require you to only buy one brand of crampons. A good guide of any stripe prioritizes the person and their experience, helping them complete their journey on their own terms and to a destination of their choosing.